What's Stopping You?

What's Stopping You?

11 Cheatcodes to Unlock the Life You Want

TIMOTHY ARMOO

PENGUIN MICHAEL JOSEPH

UK | USA | Canada | Ireland | Australia
India | New Zealand | South Africa

Penguin Michael Joseph is part of the Penguin Random House group of companies whose addresses can be found at global.penguinrandomhouse.com

Penguin Random House UK,
One Embassy Gardens, 8 Viaduct Gardens, London SW11 7BW

penguin.co.uk

First published 2026

001

Copyright © Timothy Armoo, 2026
Illustrations © Hannah Wilson, Quoted Visually, 2026

The moral right of the author has been asserted

Quotation on p. 85 by Bruce Lee reproduced by kind permission of Bruce Lee Enterprises, LLC. All rights reserved

Every effort has been made to trace copyright holders and to obtain their permission for the use of copyright material. The publisher apologizes for any errors or omissions and would be grateful to be notified of any corrections that should be incorporated in future editions of this book

Penguin Random House values and supports copyright. Copyright fuels creativity, encourages diverse voices, promotes freedom of expression and supports a vibrant culture. Thank you for purchasing an authorized edition of this book and for respecting intellectual property laws by not reproducing, scanning or distributing any part of it by any means without permission. You are supporting authors and enabling Penguin Random House to continue to publish books for everyone. No part of this book may be used or reproduced in any manner for the purpose of training artificial intelligence technologies or systems. In accordance with Article 4(3) of the DSM Directive 2019/790, Penguin Random House expressly reserves this work from the text and data mining exception

Set in 13.25/18.5pt Calluna
Typeset by Six Red Marbles UK, Thetford, Norfolk
Printed and bound in Great Britain by Clays Ltd, Elcograf S.p.A.

The authorized representative in the EEA is Penguin Random House Ireland, Morrison Chambers, 32 Nassau Street, Dublin D02 YH68

A CIP catalogue record for this book is available from the British Library

HARDBACK ISBN: 978–0–241–71922–0
TRADE PAPERBACK ISBN: 978–0–241–71927–5

Penguin Random House is committed to a sustainable future for our business, our readers and our planet. This book is made from Forest Stewardship Council® certified paper.

I dedicate this book to my parents, and to my younger self for overcoming his self-doubt.

Contents

Introduction: Why Should You Listen To Me? Or
How a Gangster Saved My Life 1
Cheatcode 1: We Are The Stories We Tell Ourselves 11
Cheatcode 2: Your Inexperience Is a Superpower 39
Cheatcode 3: Make It Easy To Win 65
Cheatcode 4: Do It Scared 91
Cheatcode 5: Originality Is Overrated 117
Cheatcode 6: Build a Network When You're a Nobody 143
Cheatcode 7: Ego is the Enemy 177
Cheatcode 8: It's Not That Deep 193
Cheatcode 9: Your Internal Scorecard 213
Cheatcode 10: How To Get Lucky 239
Cheatcode 11: Everything Big Starts Small 255

Afterword 281
Acknowledgements 285
List of Sources 287

What's Stopping You?

Introduction

Why Should You Listen To Me?
Or
How a Gangster Saved My Life

Why should you listen to me?

That's a good question. After all, there's plenty of advice out there. Plenty of gurus who'll promise you the secret to wealth and entrepreneurial success. You could choose any number of books above this one, and let's face it: one of the biggest decisions we have to make in life is where to seek advice, and who to ignore.

So: why me?

To answer that question, I want to tell you a little bit about myself.

My name is Timothy Armoo. I was born in Hackney, London. My parents weren't rich, and I was, according to my mum, an unplanned baby. Circumstances meant that my parents were not in a position to look after me. So there were two options for baby Timothy: I could either go into foster care or I could move to Ghana to live with my grandmother. After much discussion, it was decided that the second of these two options would be best for me. So, at the age of six months, I left the UK and moved to West Africa.

My grandmother was strict. I was sent to a good school where academic achievement was taken seriously, so I worked hard and won my share of classroom prizes. And although I was a long way from my parents, they too took a proper interest in my education. While I was in Ghana, my mum would send me books. In fact, she'd go so far as to head to the airport to find people who were taking flights to Accra and persuade them to deliver bundles of books to me when they landed. I liked reading the Famous Five books by Enid Blyton, and it was a joy to receive these packages. On a Sunday night, she would call on the phone and test me on the pages I was supposed to have read. From time to time, I hadn't done my homework and was forced to blag my way through her questions. Then she'd get me to spell different words out loud, which increased in complexity as I grew older, and her expectations increased. I'm so grateful now that she took the time to do this and to help me understand, even at a distance, the importance

INTRODUCTION

of language and communication. Her focus on these skills prepared me well for the future.

I always had a sense, though, that Ghana was a pit stop for me. It was not where I was meant to be, but just a chapter in the story of my life. It was no surprise when, at the age of ten, my parents decided that the time had come for me to return home to the UK. My grandmother had observed that I was becoming a little more boisterous, and it was felt that I needed to be around my parents. So I came back to live with my father.

Maybe you think that moving from Ghana to the UK meant I was going up in the world. It didn't seem like that to me at the time. In Ghana I lived in East Legon, which was a well-to-do area, the High Street Kensington of Accra. My grandmother had been the first person to move there, when it was still forest. By the time I came to live with her, she was an upper-middle-class lady living in an upper-middle-class area. My life in Ghana was relatively privileged. My life in the UK, when I returned in 2005, was definitely not.

My father lived on the Old Kent Road on a rough council estate. This was not the slightly posh surroundings of East Legon. I quickly appreciated the lesson learned by many immigrants: your money goes a lot further in a city like Accra than it does in a city like London. My new home was many steps up a bleak concrete staircase, and many steps down the social scale. More importantly, it quickly became apparent to me that I had arrived in a part of London that was at the height of gang warfare. There were three crews: Old Kent Road, Peckham and Brixton. The nexus of their gang warfare was Avondale Square, right next to where I lived.

The gang violence was real. You couldn't avoid it. Like all young people, I wanted to be part of a group. My dad was always working, which meant I was often left to my own devices. I craved a sense of community, and I started to find it with the Old Kent Road crew. I told myself that this was what community meant, what family meant, what brotherhood meant. I told myself that if I wanted any kind of credibility in the world in which I found myself, I needed to be accepted by the rappers and the gangsters, by the guys with hoodies, bandanas and knives. These thoughts inevitably started to inform the way I acted, and the path my life started to take.

There was a football cage in Avondale Square. I remember one day playing football there with my friends when somebody in the cage shouted out: 'Peckham boys!' I looked beyond the cage and saw a bunch of lads approaching, some on foot, some on their bikes, wearing

INTRODUCTION

bandanas and hoodies. They were a range of ages. The older boys were more battle-hardened. The younger ones had something to prove and wanted to show that they, too, were hard men. All of them hurried towards us, and it was completely clear that they didn't want a game of football. They were looking for trouble. My friends and I dispersed from the cage. We ran. Fast. One of the Peckham boys caught up with me. He had a knife. He swung it across my abdomen, missing me by inches. I sprinted to the safety of my friend's house, horribly aware of what might have happened had that boy been a step closer to me.

The school I went to – City of London Academy in Southwark – was situated on the border of Old Kent Road, Peckham and Brixton. It meant that kids from all three gangs were under the same roof. During the week, everyone seemed to get along. At the weekend, everyone became mortal enemies. One day I went to school and a friend of mine was absent. 'Haven't you heard?' one of my schoolmates said. 'He was in McDonald's and someone stabbed him.' Sure enough, my friend had an ugly scar all the way up his right side from the encounter. He was lucky to be alive.

This was the environment in which I found myself. The path I had started to tread. I was 13 years old, however, when my English teacher Miss Sobaki took me to one side. She could see what was happening, and she wanted to intervene. 'Timothy,' she said, 'you realize you're a smart guy, right? This bad man stuff, it's not for you.'

I'll always be grateful to Miss Sobaki. Her words hit home. I took on board what she said, and she helped me change the way I thought about myself. My desire to be a bad man started to wane, but my urge to be part of a community was still strong. In the end, it took a gangster to divert me fully from that path. It took a gangster to save my life.

I was at the house of one of the guys in the Old Kent Road crew, with a bunch of other gang members. They were preparing to 'ride out'. Riding out is when one gang ventures on to the turf of another, with the aim of doing two things. Firstly, to create a video on the other gang's territory, to goad them by gloating that their turf has been infiltrated. And secondly, to stab someone. The prospect terrified me. As much as I wanted to be part of this community, I was very much on the periphery of what was happening. I wanted nothing to do with the violence. As they prepared to ride out, one of the older gang members took me to one side and shook his head. 'Bro,' he said, 'this shit isn't for you.' He could tell that

INTRODUCTION

my heart wasn't in it, any more than my head was. He knew me from school: the quiet, smart, bookish kid who was more interested in intellectual pursuits than gang-related ones. He knew that riding out was not for me.

I can still recall the relief I felt when that boy gave me permission to alter the way I thought about myself. Now I realize he taught me an important lesson, though I doubt he knew it. So many people zombie their way through life, putting up with a job they don't like or a relationship that isn't working, and waiting for external permission to change by a perceived authority figure. We think of permission as being something we need to kick-start an activity. Sometimes, though, we find ourselves waiting for permission to stop. I didn't ride out with the gang that day, or any other day. Once I had permission to stop being the gangster I didn't really want to be, my life started to change.

I'll tell you more about how that change happened in the next chapter. For now, let's fast forward. At the age of 21, in my second year of university and after a few failures and successes in the world of business, I founded a company called Fanbytes. Fanbytes was an influencer marketing agency that helped brands like Nike, Samsung and even the UK Government win the hearts of Gen Z. In six years, I took the company from zero to 80 people and a highly publicized eight-figure acquisition. It meant I became rich beyond my wildest dreams before I'd even reached the age of 30. *Huffington Post* named me their Entrepreneur of the Year. I became the face of *Forbes* 30 under 30. I travelled the world speaking on global stages to the likes of Goldman Sachs, Adobe and Dell about the new world of media. My content on social media, in which I offer advice for entrepreneurs, reached millions of people.

My path, though, could have been very different. If it hadn't been for Miss Sobaki and the gangster who saved my life, who knows where I might have ended up? Even with their help, I certainly didn't see people like me represented in business as I worked my way up. Kids from the Old Kent Road weren't supposed to get rich. If it was going to happen, I'd have to figure it out for myself.

And that's why I think you should listen to me.

I don't know everything. It's not like I've found the secret to life and, like everyone, I'm still learning. But the title of this book is *What's Stopping You?* All too often, the answer is that in business – and in life – the elements that really move the needle are the things that more experienced people don't tell you. Why would they, when it would give you an unfair advantage over them? I call these elements the cheatcodes. They're programmed

INTRODUCTION

in, but hidden under bland advice to pay your dues, wait your turn and stay in your lane. In other words: advice to hold you back.

I didn't want to hold myself back, and I don't think you should either. I don't think you should let *anything* stop you, so I want to help you hack the system. That's why I'm sharing the cheatcodes with you. I want to tell you everything I wish I'd known at the age of 21, to help you aim bigger, stand firm, fight for the life – and the wealth – you want and go all in.

These cheatcodes have been hard won from first-hand experience on the front line of entrepreneurship, and let me tell you: they are not quick fixes. A cheatcode is not an easy win or a shortcut. Success in business is almost always the result of hard work, determination and resilience. Don't ever forget that. Too often, though, I find people hindered by a lack of self-belief – an 'I can't do it' attitude – and it's this that prevents them from starting in the first place. Perhaps you recognize that trait in yourself. Perhaps you believe you don't know enough about business to take the first step. Perhaps you're overwhelmed by the thought of pivoting in your career. Perhaps you don't have the confidence to take the next step towards fulfilling your ambition, whatever it may be. If that's the case, I hope you'll find in the cheatcodes the key to unlocking the next stage in your journey. I hope they'll be the kickstart you've been looking for.

There is a narrative that success in business is the domain of a certain type of person, and it's very easy to accept that narrative. We need to challenge it if we are to democratize success, which leads us directly to our first cheatcode. It's something I learned very early, not long after that gangster saved my life, and it is this: we are the stories we tell ourselves.

Cheatcode 1: We Are The Stories We Tell Ourselves

As a young teenager living with my dad, I always assumed that he worked in property management. I'd see letters around the flat from his employers, Southwark Homecare. It made sense to me that he should have a good, well-paying job. He had been to a high-achieving boys' school in Ghana, and then on to university at the Sorbonne in Paris. Academia was the path to financial success, or so I thought. This was certainly the message I'd received in Ghana. So I assumed that even though we lived four flights up on a shitty council estate, we were OK financially.

Gradually, though, I started to doubt my assumption about my dad's job. I heard him use phrases like 'on call', and talking about working extra hours. This didn't seem to me like the language of a property management person. One afternoon, when I was 15 and sitting alone in my bedroom, it hit me. My dad wasn't in property management at all. He worked in social care. I knew that this was not a high-paying job. Suddenly our humble living circumstances made a lot more sense. Social work is a noble and important profession, no doubt, but I remember thinking that it was perhaps not the lucrative career my dad might have expected to enter, given his level of education. And I remember saying to myself that very afternoon: I am going to be the one who takes us to the next level, financially speaking.

We lived on the top floor of our council block, and the building had no lift so we had to climb the stairs, which was a bit of a drag. At times it felt dangerous, being a young Black boy coming home from school in winter, when it was dark outside and the stairwell was gloomy, and there were often undesirable characters hanging round the estate. Anything could happen. In retrospect, though, I'm pleased I was forced to climb those stairs. As I hurried up that stairwell, trying to avoid trouble, scared and a little bit disappointed by my environment, I repeated a mantra in my head with each step. *I don't belong here. I'm meant for more. I don't belong here. I'm meant for more . . .*

It became, I think, a mild form of OCD. I couldn't climb that staircase without repeating the mantra. And the more I repeated it, the more I altered my internal story. By repeatedly stating my mantra, I grew to believe it. The more I believed it, the more I lived it. In the quiet of my bedroom, I would open up my little Toshiba laptop and I would write motivating messages to myself. *It's OK, Timothy. One day all this will change, and you'll be the catalyst for that change.* I didn't know what journalling was at the time, but I suppose this was my fledgling version of that. I turned the flickering cursor into the story I wanted to believe about myself.

And, little by little, I became that story.

It's easy to imagine that everyone's lives are merely a function of their external influences. That we are who we are because of the circumstances into which we were born and the cards that life deals us.

My experience suggests that this is not completely true.

Don't get me wrong. A kid brought up in poverty might well encounter more difficulties than a kid brought up in privilege. There are factors of wealth, class, race, gender and opportunity that shape our lives and predict our outcomes.

But that's not the whole story. It is not only external factors that define who we are.

As I discovered when I climbed the stairs of that

council block and sat in my bedroom with my little Toshiba laptop, we have the power to shape our internal monologues. We have the power to mould the way we think about ourselves in order to become the person we want to be and achieve the goals we dream of.

In short, we are the stories we tell ourselves. These stories, properly harnessed, are incredibly powerful. More powerful, I would argue, than factors of circumstance, because they literally allow us to become different people.

In this chapter, I'm going to tell you how I went from being that kid on the Old Kent Road with few prospects, to being the founder of a multi-million-pound company. I did this, in part, by harnessing the power of this cheatcode to alter the narrative of my life and consequently define its outcome. I hope that in sharing parts of my story, I'll inspire you to shape the path of your own life in a way that is meaningful and impactful for you. And I hope that, along the way, you'll pick up a few tips about how to adopt a mindset that is conducive to success in the world of business and entrepreneurship.

Retire at 21

I was only a teenager. I couldn't yet change my physical surroundings, but I was beginning to understand that I could change my mental surroundings. Now that I was no longer associating so much with the Old Kent Road boys, I had time to read and research, to flesh out my story and my plans. I stumbled across a website called 'Retire at 21'. It contained articles about all sorts of people who had built successful businesses and become financially independent at a young age. As I read about these founders and entrepreneurs, I realized that there was a world in which their stories were possible. I made it my mission to immerse myself in those stories. Every day when I got home from school, I'd log on to that website and others like it. I would read about people who had built their own businesses, familiarizing myself with a different category of person to those I saw around me in my daily life. I read and I read and I read, not only because I wanted to know about the entrepreneurship displayed by these people whose successes I aspired to emulate, but also because I wanted to normalize the idea of success in my mind. As I read, I thought to myself: I want to do that. I *can* do that.

Those men and women who have done it before are no different to me. *That is the sort of person I am.*

I think we readily accept the notion that negative internal narratives have a negative effect on our outlook and wellbeing. They make us act differently. The reverse is true for positive narratives, as I discovered. The story I told myself became reality. I gradually became the person I visualized, to the extent that now I am acquainted with many of the people I read about as a kid on those websites.

> Repeating mantras to yourself is a powerful way to help you change the way you think. There is evidence to suggest that, as well as improving cognitive function, repeating mantras can lead to structural changes in the brain. They can be an effective shortcut to changing the stories we tell ourselves.

The £500 Mercedes

You never know when your journey into entrepreneurship will start. For me, it started with a bet when I was 14 years old.

WE ARE THE STORIES WE TELL OURSELVES

I had a good friend called Kunal. We were walking home from school one day when we passed a fancy black Mercedes parked in the street. 'How much do you think it's worth?' Kunal asked me.

I shrugged. 'Five hundred pounds?' Truth was, I didn't really know, but £500 was a substantial sum to us at the time and felt like the right amount of money for such an object of desire.

'I bet you,' Kunal said, 'that you'll never have five hundred pounds in your pocket before you turn eighteen.'

I didn't like the idea that this might be true. I was obsessed with stories of people who'd made far more than that in far shorter periods of time. I took the bet and went home to start planning how I could win it. I'll explain what happened next later in this book, but I mention Kunal here because he also consolidated in my mind the idea that we are the stories we tell ourselves. I realized that, in normalizing the idea that I could be a successful entrepreneur, I had altered my response to the idea that I wasn't the type of person who could make money. Kunal hadn't done this. Don't get me wrong: he was a very smart guy. Smarter than me. We would compete for grades, and he was the only person in the school who routinely scored higher than I did. Not only was he off-the-charts brainy, he was also super hard-working. There is no doubt that he had the intellectual tools to make it in the world of business. From time to time over the years I would try to get him involved in my entrepreneurial schemes. But he had no real interest in that. He was not a risk-taker, whereas I had internalized the idea that I was exactly that. So Kunal went off to Imperial College London to study for a degree in physics. He saw himself as an academic, not an entrepreneur. That was the story he told himself, so that's the person he became.

Many years later, when Kunal and I had lost touch, I was walking through a park in London. I saw a bench with a name inscribed on a plaque: Kunal Patel. I made enquiries and learned that he had recently died. Now, every time I walk or cycle past that park, I make a little nod in the direction of that bench, and I silently tell Kunal that I love him. His challenge that day was the kickstart I needed to start becoming the version of myself that I knew I could be.

Act like the person you want to become

I realized that changing my environment, albeit temporarily, would be an important tool when it came to changing my story. It's difficult to keep telling yourself a story of success when you're surrounded by the pound shops, fried-chicken joints and rain-streaked concrete of a south London council estate. I wanted to be a successful entrepreneur, but would a successful entrepreneur be working out of a steamy cafe? Would they be sitting on the edge of their bed in a dingy council estate flat? They would not. I decided I should act like the version of my future self that I hoped to be and find myself a more appropriate place to work.

I settled upon Claridge's, one of the poshest hotels in the world, playground of the wealthy and successful.

I picked out my best clothes. A horrendous pair of brown chinos from BHS. A white T-shirt from Sports Direct. A dark-blue blazer from Asda, by far the smartest garment I owned. Some blue loafers. Cheap tech-bro chic. These were not the threads of a poor boy from the Old Kent Road. Granted, nor were they the threads of a City millionaire. But they were the best I had, and by choosing them I achieved two objectives: I helped deal with the anxiety that a scruffy Black boy from a poor part of town would be swiftly shown the exit the moment he tried to walk into a swanky hotel, and I made a commitment to taking myself seriously. Because if *I* didn't take myself seriously, nobody else would. Putting on those clothes was like putting on a uniform. They helped me become a new person.

The very first day I walked through the door of Claridge's, I knew I'd made the right call. The doorman called me 'sir'. Nobody called me 'sir' in south London! It made me feel important, like I had a right to be there, like I was there to do proper business like a proper businessman. The surroundings in the foyer were comfortable, even plush. There was a chequerboard floor and richly upholstered chairs and tables. In Claridge's, I was surrounded by successful, wealthy people, by men and women who had 'made it' and among whom I needed to feel comfortable if I was to become one of their number. Back home, the landings outside our flats were lined with aunties who gossiped, smoked and stared out into the distance. What were they doing with their lives? I didn't know, but it was anathema to a kid like me, driven by a sense of purpose. In Claridge's, even the air was different. It smelled sweet and clean. Back home, the air was hot and dirty and dusty. It did you no good to breathe it in.

WE ARE THE STORIES WE TELL OURSELVES

The process of walking into Claridge's in my work outfit changed my mindset. Eventually, after I'd gone there several times, I ended up on first-name terms with the doorman, Ian. It felt cool for him to welcome me by name into the hotel, and it transformed my sense of who I was. Instead of being an anxious kid from the Old Kent Road, I gradually developed an alter ego. By *telling* myself that I was a different person, I *became* that person. I belonged to the world into which I'd inserted myself.

> Be your future self.
> Visualize the version of yourself that exists 12 months from now.
> The one that achieved everything you set out to do.
> See it clearly.
> Take that version from the future and 'inject' it into your current body with your current circumstances.
> Now play the game from his/her eyes.

Tim 'The Rules Don't Apply' Armoo

Visiting Claridge's taught me the power of changing your environment if you want to change your story. At the age of 16, an opportunity came my way to change my environment even further. I was offered scholarships to three different private schools: Dulwich College, Alleyn's and Christ's Hospital. Dulwich and Alleyn's were probably the better schools. I chose to become a boarder at Christ's Hospital. It could not have been more different to the inner-city state school I'd known previously. Here, the students were expected to wear a fancy school uniform. A marching band played us into the dining hall for lunch every day (seriously!). We were not surrounded by the bleak concrete of Peckham and the Old Kent Road, but by grand architecture and green playing fields. There was no knife crime in this genteel corner of West Sussex.

It was not my natural habitat.

I knew I might struggle to fit in, but I was never in any doubt that this change in circumstance was the right thing for me. In fact, I made a conscious effort to ensure that my new circumstances were as different as possible. That was the reason I chose this school above the others. Christ's Hospital represented a far greater change in geography and environment. It took me out of my previous life and into a genuinely new chapter of the story I was writing for myself. It didn't just offer me a completely new physical environment. It offered me a completely new mental environment too.

It was difficult, at first, being a south London council estate boy in this posh and exclusive school. I didn't quite fit in. But it was not really the colour of my skin or the demographic of my background that made me different. It was a question of attitude. I made friends with a white middle-class boy called Sam, and he had a name for me: Tim 'The Rules Don't Apply' Armoo. We were expected to be in bed with our lights out by ten o'clock. I never obeyed. Why should I, when I was always reading at night? We were expected to congregate for our march into lunch at one o'clock. I was always late. We were expected to be clean-shaven, but I grew a beard. Having the build of a rugby winger, I was told I was on the team. I refused, and the occasional punishment came my way. For example, I was suspended for getting drunk on my 18th birthday. However, it became apparent to me that the punishments I received were not as severe as I might have expected. I was never *properly* disciplined.

I believe that the reason for that was the story I told myself. Years later my housemaster, having seen a newspaper article about me, sent me a lovely message. He observed that, although I could never quite bring myself to follow the rules, he always knew I had the potential to make something of myself. I realized then that when I moved out of my comfort zone to Christ's Hospital, I made an active choice to project my internal narrative, and *this made people treat me differently*. The stories we tell ourselves do not only define who we are, they define how other people see us.

A category of one

There exists in business a powerful idea about being in a category of one. Rather than trying to compete against a whole bunch of people, the category of one paradigm suggests that you should find a field where there is not much competition and dominate in that field. When I made the transition from south London to Christ's Hospital, I realized that I was going to have to tell myself a new story, if I hoped to be in a category of one among my peers.

As a young teenager, the identity I built for myself centred on academic success. I'd done well at school in Ghana, where academia was everything. My English teacher had warned me off gang culture by telling me I was too smart to get involved. Kunal and I had competed for the best grades. I became a bookworm, always in the library, always reading, always learning something new. The story I told myself was this: I was the smart one. I had a good brain. When it came to academia, I could hold my own with anyone.

Then I moved to Christ's Hospital. All of a sudden, I found myself in the company of genuine geniuses, people for whom it was unthinkable that they would not go to Oxford or Cambridge, people who, from the perspective of raw computation, had brains that simply worked faster than mine. I didn't think that I could easily win the game of being the smartest guy in their company, and I didn't think I cared enough about it to put in the extra effort anyway. But there were other ways for me to put myself in a category of one. I decided that I could win the game of being the entrepreneurial one. I told myself that story, and then I went about fulfilling it. I started a newspaper called *Entrepreneur Express*. I founded a school public-speaking competition. I decided to win the entrepreneurial game rather than the academic game, and by successfully doing so I learned an important lesson. We can not only choose the game we want to win, we can *create* the game we want to win. You might not be the brightest person in your job, you might not be the funniest person in the office, but you might be more spreadsheet-inclined than anyone else. Own it. Take pride in being the spreadsheet person. Create the game you want to win, then win it really well.

If you create your own story, you put yourself in pole position to be the hero of that story.

The alter ego

There is power in developing an alter ego. Many years later, when I was running Fanbytes, I was asked to do a public-speaking engagement. I'd done a few of these things before, but this was the biggest yet. There was an audience of 4,000 people, and my talk was to be broadcast on TV. When I'd agreed to do it, I had no idea that it was quite such a prestigious, large-scale event. I simply thought it might be an opportunity to publicize the company and maybe gain a few customers.

As I stood in the wings waiting to deliver my talk, I felt incredibly anxious. This was well out of my comfort zone. I tried to get my head in the right space, to hype myself up and master my anxiety. I said to myself: there is someone in the world for whom giving a speech in front of 4,000 people is absolutely nothing. How can I become that person? As I was trying to work this out, a lady approached me. I can see her now, with her blonde hair and her pink shirt. She said, 'How do you want to be introduced? Is it Tim, is it Timothy, is it Timo?'

Up until that point, the only people who had called me Timo had been my dad and my grandma. Nobody else had used that version of my name. Now I thought: Timo sounds kind of cool! Maybe Timo is that guy who finds it easy to talk in front of 4,000 people. Maybe Timo is that guy who doesn't need to hype himself up beforehand. So I said, 'Sure, call me Timo.' As soon as I adopted that new personality, I felt the anxiety recede. This new name was not so different from the dark-blue Asda jacket I wore to Claridge's. It helped me to understand that I did not always have to be the person I'd always been, and to believe that I was the person I wanted to be. It helped me change the story I told myself.

This idea of creating a new public-facing persona is tried and tested. People in the public eye, especially music artists, do it all the time. They invent a new self, and that self is the personality they project. I'm a Drake fan. Drake is his middle name. In 'real life' he's Aubrey Graham, and I don't doubt that those two people are very different individuals. The Weeknd, Elton John, Ziggy

Stardust – these are all alter egos for artists who undergo a transformation of persona to help them present a particular version of themselves to the world; the different characters they create in the story of their lives.

There is no world in which this doesn't happen . . .

This technique has real, practical value in the world of business and entrepreneurship where we often find ourselves having to perform seemingly outrageous tasks that are not normally part of our everyday life.

Part of the process of building a successful startup is fundraising. When a company reaches a stage where it needs to expand, it costs money. That money needs to come from somewhere, and so it is the role of the founders to seek investment. This means you find yourself in front of very wealthy individuals, asking for substantial sums. Think *Dragons' Den*.

The first time I had to do this, I was young and green. My pitch for £15,000 was to an investor called Nick Wheeler, the founder of Charles Tyrwhitt shirts, who had agreed to invest in certain student startups. I made the pitch along with my co-founder, Ambrose, and I memorized every word of the pitch so that I could deliver it perfectly. I realized, though, that a perfect delivery was not enough. I had to project a certain confidence, and to do this it was necessary to release myself from the anxiety that the pitch might not be successful. The story I told myself was twofold. Firstly, I told myself that there was no world in which Nick did not give us this money. It *had* to happen, and it *would* happen. Secondly, I told myself that *somebody* had to receive this money from Nick. Why shouldn't it be us? This was a conscious psychological shift. Just as when I walked into the foyer of Claridge's telling myself that I deserved to be there, so I walked into that meeting telling myself that I had every right to expect a successful outcome. The alternative was not part of my story.

Later in my journey, I had to raise much greater sums of money, but having deployed this technique on a smaller scale, I now had the confidence to deploy it on a grander one. Asking for half a million pounds from a guy I've never met before? Bring it on. There is no world in which that doesn't happen.

> The day you realize that almost anything you want is more attainable than you think, your world will shift.
>
> The body you want is more attainable than you think.
>
> The career you want is more attainable than you think.
>
> The bank balance you want is more attainable than you think.
>
> Internalize this.

Define the person you want to be

Becoming the stories we tell ourselves is an ongoing process. Sometimes it can be a scary process too.

There comes a point in any business when it becomes clear that the business is going to work. For me, this came after a year of Fanbytes. We'd made £400,000, we knew we were providing a service that people wanted and customers were paying us. I realized at that point that it was now down to me to decide how big the business was going to be. How hard was I prepared to work? What type of person was I prepared to be in order to make it as successful as possible?

At the time we were a company of eight people. I realized the company would have to grow to 40 or 50 people. We would have to go after bigger clients. We would have to raise more money from investors. We were at an inflection point, where a small-time business was transitioning into a big-time business, and it was down to me to make it happen. At that point, I was fearful. I knew I would have to become the kind of CEO who understood more about hiring, managing and leading people, about landing big customers, about fundraising and organizational structures. Problem was, I was only 21 and I didn't know any of this shit. It scared me, but I came to realize that I wasn't scared of failure. I was scared of success. Because in order to be successful, I would have to be a different person and I didn't know if I had the skills, the habits or the discipline to become that person.

I had to tell myself a new story: that there existed, somewhere, a 21-year-old for whom this situation was normal and completely within their sphere of expertise. I had to work out how to become that person.

Sometimes to have something you've never had, you have to become someone you've never been. It can be hard to be that person you've never been if you think of him or her as merely an extension of your current self. 'It's me, but I work harder.' You have to take yourself into a new dimension, to be a new person with new disciplines and new mindsets. You must define, in painstaking detail, who this new person is, because you can't reach your destination if you don't know your direction of travel. Write it down on a piece of paper. What are the characteristics of the person you need to be? How does that person spend his or her time? What is important to them? Who do they associate with? Where do they hang out? How do they talk? I never used to speak the way I speak now. I was less measured and less articulate. I dropped my Ts, like any other kid from a south London council estate. When I wrote down my list of characteristics, I realized that the person I wanted to be took much greater care of his language. Our words and our speech define us. If we change our words, we change our stories.

Once you have defined the person you want to be, you start inching towards becoming that person. This is significantly less simple than it sounds. It requires incremental steps. Perhaps the person you want to be is an early riser. For a few weeks, the only characteristic of your future self that you need to manifest is to get up early. Don't worry about anything else. Action that one tiny step and only move on to the next when it has become second nature to you.

I did exactly this to overcome a much bigger issue than oversleeping. When I was younger, I struggled with a fairly significant stutter. I realized that, as CEO of Fanbytes, I would have to go out to conferences and events, and talk to people about why influencer marketing matters. My co-founders and I had to become thought leaders, and that meant communicating with others. I realized that, although I had told myself many positive stories about who I was and who I wanted to be, one story that I continued to tell myself was this: I am a person who stutters, which means public speaking is going to be very difficult for me. So I wrote on my list that in order for Fanbytes to work, I needed to become a better public speaker.

In one of our early offices, we had a breakout space with a small stage. I would wait until nine or ten o'clock at night, when everybody else had gone home, and as soon as I knew nobody else could hear me, I'd stand up on the stage and rehearse giving big, stutter-free presentations. Then I initiated stand-up presentations in our basement office in Shoreditch, just me and my eight employees. Those presentations were complete overkill – I could just as easily have discussed the matters we covered with people over lunch – but that wasn't the point. Those presentations occurred solely so that I could gradually become comfortable with public speaking on a small scale, so anxiety did not make my stutter kick in when I had to speak on a larger scale.

Changing the stories we tell ourselves is not just an internal mental process. It's a process of slowly changing our actions and behaviours into those of the person we want to become.

> How to get something you've never had:
> Be OK with destroying who you currently are.
> Ask yourself if your current habits, consumption and thoughts will lead to who you want to become.
> This is a painful process.
> But it's why few will actually do it.

The Steven Spielberg strategy

The strategy of becoming the stories we tell ourselves is not new or original. This is not a maverick way of thinking cooked up by a kid from a council estate. It's a time-honoured technique of successful people from all walks of life.

As a 12-year-old boy, the film director Steven Spielberg used to imagine himself accepting an Oscar and thanking the Academy. In doing so, he was employing a psychological modality called 'mental rehearsal', which is the process of telling yourself a story so that you can bring an imagined future into your present. Spielberg knew what he wanted his future to hold. Life just had to catch up. Walt Disney would practise his signature ad nauseam when he was an ambitious child. He told himself that he was going to need it.

The technique is particularly common in the world of high-performance sports. I'm inspired by the NBA basketball player Kobe Bryant, who spoke movingly about the power of rewriting his own narrative. Michael Jordan would tell himself stories about what other people were saying about him and, whether they were true or not, use them to motivate himself. Sports psychology in general is all about athletes reframing the stories they tell themselves about their abilities and potential. It's a technique that can serve us well in our wider lives.

Visualize the destination

Many of us have a good idea of what our end destination is. We know we can reach that destination, but the only thing blocking our way is ourselves. We know that the job we want, the relationship we want or the business we want is perfectly achievable, but our sense of self limits us.

We need to be adaptable, while never losing sight of that destination. On the Fanbytes journey, there were many obstacles along the way. When the Snapchat algorithm changed in a way that compromised our approach, we seriously considered becoming an e-commerce company and selling socks online. But I never lost sight of the destination I set myself: to have a successful business exit by the time I was 30 years old. It gave me a solid foundation for everything else I wanted to do in my life. After we sold the company, I was often asked, 'Did you think this would happen?' My response was always the same: 'It's exactly as I designed it.' I was talking about the destination, not the journey. Just as Steven Spielberg would practise his Oscar acceptance speech in his bedroom mirror, or a painter might visualize their finished work of art, I would mentally rehearse the endgame of refreshing my Santander bank account and seeing that I had more money than I ever thought possible when I was sitting in my bedroom on the Old Kent Road. There is value to making that visualization as real and visceral as you can, and revisiting it frequently.

We are the stories we tell ourselves, and the best stories are vivid and colourful. And while the route to success often changes, repeating the story we tell ourselves about our destination is a powerful tool in helping us arrive there.

The Cheat Sheet

- We have the power to change our internal monologues. We can't become the person we want to be, unless we tell ourselves that person is possible.
- Other people are part of our story. By presenting ourselves as the person we want to be, we affect the way others treat us.
- We can not only choose the game we want to win, we can *create* the game we want to win.

- By defining the characteristics of our future self, we can take incremental steps to becoming that self.
- Visualizing our destination – the successful conclusion of our story – allows us to keep our eye on the prize, even when the journey changes.

Cheatcode 2: Your Inexperience Is a Superpower

When I was 17, I sold a website for £110,000.

Inspired by the entrepreneurial websites I'd been addicted to for years, I decided to launch a magazine called *Entrepreneur Express*. My intention was to release a print version and an online version. The print version failed pretty quickly, so I found myself having to work out the best way of directing traffic to the online version. I tried Google Ads but realized they were expensive. I tried SEO but it failed. I was at my wits' end. How was I, a schoolboy, going to get eyeballs on the website when all these other competitors in the space, like *Business Insider* and *Forbes,* were so much bigger and better funded than me? They could just squash me. I needed to figure out an edge.

Then I realized I already had an edge. Like every other young person at the time, I was spending hours every day on Facebook. I *lived* on Facebook. I understood this social platform better than my competitors. *Business Insider* and *Forbes* saw social platforms as a complementary thing. Because I was young, I understood their full potential.

I figured that I could get certain fast-growing Facebook pages to post some of my content and send traffic back. It worked immediately. So, I started creating my own Facebook pages about business and motivation, posted my content there and drove traffic back to my site in return. I knew that the audience was out there on Facebook, and my approach seemed logical and intuitive. But it only felt logical and intuitive because I was young, and this was the landscape in which I operated. I doubt that a 50-something would have had even a fraction of that understanding. They would not have been able to do what I did.

Too often, in business and in life, inexperience is framed as a disadvantage. It's not. Inexperience can be a superpower.

It's easy to miss this concept when you're young. Certainly, I took my youth for granted at the time. I didn't fully understand the advantages that it offered. I think it's common for young, inexperienced people to compare themselves unfavourably to older, more experienced, better-connected individuals. It's a mistake, because everything you think you don't have can be reframed as an advantage.

In this chapter I'd like to persuade you to embrace exactly those things that you might think mean you're not ready. But this is not just a chapter for young people. I also hope to persuade you that it's possible to harness some of these ideas even when you're older.

Be naive

Entrepreneur Express was my second business. I started my first when I was just 14. Remember my friend Kunal who bet me that I'd never earn £500 to buy a Mercedes before the age of 18? I naively took that bet. How hard could it be, I thought to myself, to set up a little enterprise of my own? My youthful assumption that I was up to the challenge had not yet been tempered with a dose of reality about how hard it can sometimes be to persuade people to pay you money.

I came up with a plan. I was known at my school in Bermondsey as someone who was good at maths. Now, you may be under the impression from what you know about my upbringing that being a maths nerd might not have been considered a good thing at that school. You'd be wrong. There were plenty of aspirational kids and, crucially for me, plenty of kids from Asian backgrounds whose parents prized success in mathematics. If these kids weren't making the grade, they'd come to me for help. I realized I had a natural ability that I could monetize, and so I started charging.

At first, a trigonometry session with 14-year-old Timothy would set you back £10. There seemed to be a market for it, so after a week I increased my rate to £15. I had a number of satisfied clients, for whom I was able to unravel the mysteries of algebra, and so I received enquiries about other subjects. Could I help people out with physics, chemistry and biology? As I was decent at maths, physics was in my wheelhouse. Chemistry at that level was not too difficult. But biology? Biology didn't interest me. It wasn't where my expertise lay. So I thought to myself: how do I service this gap in the market if I myself don't want to teach biology? I came up with a simple answer. Every six weeks we would do an end-of-module test in each subject. All I needed to do was find out who'd done best in the most recent biology test, and see if they would like to become a tutor for my fledgling business. I approached our teacher, asked who was the star biology pupil, and she told me. I wandered down to the library, saw the student and popped the question: 'Do you want to earn some money?'

I knew that the answer to that question would be yes. The answer to that question was *always* yes. So I made him a proposition: £10 an hour to tutor biology if I supplied the students. I charged the client £15 and the bit in the middle, £5, was my profit.

When I look back on those first steps into the world of business, it strikes me that I was very naive. That naivety helped. I wonder how somebody with a good deal of life experience might have approached the same situation. Would they have taken such a direct approach, or would they have put obstacles in their way as they trod a more traditional path? Would they have worried that the teacher would be concerned with issues of privacy, or that they might have reservations about students tutoring other students? Perhaps they'd be taking a more convoluted route, putting out flyers and hoping that tutors would come to them. They would likely shun the naive approach, because nobody in later life wants to be considered naive.

When you're inexperienced, however, naivety works because the simple approach is often the best.

When everything is new, nothing is unusual

The naive approach translated directly to Fanbytes. My co-founders and I were inexperienced and had very little idea of the accepted way of going about things. It led to a first-principles mindset, much like my approach to the biology teacher.

We had no real idea about how the social-media world worked. We didn't realize that our competitors were charging a cost per follower or a cost according to the size of the influencers. Had we known that, maybe we'd have done the same. Instead, we naively thought: brands are paying for actual engagement, so why not charge them based on that and adopt a business model of cost per view. It turned out to be a good idea.

In the second year of Fanbytes, we naively failed to understand fully the significance of having the government as a client. The first campaign we did with them in 2018 came about because there was a new minimum wage. A lot of young people didn't know about it, so the government came to us because of a talk I'd done, to ask if we'd create a Snapchat campaign to promote the policy. No problem. We ran the campaign, it did well, and the government became a regular client. It was only during our final funding round in 2021, when I happened to mention that we had the UK Government as a client, that I fully realized its importance. I mentioned it in passing and received a slightly sceptical double-take from one of the potential investors. 'You have the UK Government as a client?' Sure. It didn't seem like a big deal to us. Had we known the importance of that contract at the very beginning, perhaps we would have freaked out a little and put obstacles in our path. Perhaps we'd have overplayed our hand. A more experienced entrepreneur might reasonably have taken the position that a bunch of youngsters like us would never have landed such a serious contract. But not us, because when you don't know what's impossible, you act like everything is possible.

Young people are on the crest of a wave

Inexperience goes hand in hand with youth. The world changes fast and young people often find themselves on the crest of that wave. I benefited from this when I made a success of *Entrepreneur Express.* Here are some other examples of young people whose success has, in part, been a product of their youth because they had a better understanding of the world in which their contemporaries operate.

Ben Francis

As a kid, Ben Francis was obsessed with fitness and IT. It meant he was plugged in to the burgeoning gym culture and fashion trends of young people, as well as their evolving use of technology and mobile platforms. While he was still at school he developed two bestselling fitness apps. By the age of 20, he had segued into the fitness clothing website Gymshark. It wouldn't have mattered much if he'd failed, because he was so young. And because he was young, he knew what young people wanted. Crucially, he fully understood Instagram, and its potential for low-cost influencer marketing, by dint of being a young person. Today, Ben Francis is a dollar billionaire.

Isaac Medeiros

Isaac Medeiros founded a company called Mini Katana in his early twenties. Mini Katana sells Japanese swords online. Isaac is a millionaire many times over because he instinctively understood how to make videos of his swords go viral on Instagram and TikTok. He knew that young people would be there for videos of the swords slicing cleanly through watermelons and performing other gonzo stunts, and was able to translate those viral videos into sales. This all happened because he was immersed in the language and culture of social media in a way that an older person might not have been. He was, if you'll excuse the pun, at the cutting edge.

Amika George

As a teenager, Amika George became concerned with the issue of period poverty. At the age of 17 she kickstarted a petition that gathered 200,000 signatories. While still at school she founded the organization #FreePeriods and successfully petitioned the UK Government to provide free sanitary products to poor young people. She was appointed an MBE for her services to education. Because she was young, Amika had a deep understanding of the concerns and preoccupations of her contemporaries. She understood that young people cared about period poverty, and was able to harness that understanding in an incredibly impactful way. (Amika's story is also a great example of how youthful naivety can effect real change, where a cynical older person might assume that the hurdles would be too difficult to jump.)

Young people often imagine that older people will not take them seriously. Perhaps that's sometimes true in general life. In the entrepreneurial space, the foolishness of dismissing young people has long since been discarded. If there's a chance you're going to make someone money, trust me: they'll take you seriously. When you're young, you're an expert in youth. When older people want to know what's next, what's coming up, what's trending, your expertise is invaluable to them. That means your youth is a massive advantage.

> As a young person, you might think you don't have skills, when you actually have many. Take a sheet of paper and write out a list of what comes easy to you that comes harder to other people. You'll find out that it's a lot more than you think. Maybe you understand TikTok better than the average person. Maybe you have a natural flair for product management. Perhaps you're good at integrating online elements using Webflow. Perhaps you

> happen to be very good at Canva. The skills you have will undoubtedly be of value to somebody who lacks them.

You have fewer boats to burn

There is a rhetoric on social media that encourages entrepreneurs to 'burn the boats'. It means that you should quit your job and go all-in on your business idea, so that you have the extra motivation to succeed. I think it's one of the dumbest pieces of advice I've ever heard. Businesses fail all the time. If the cost of failure is that you can't make the rent or pay the gas bill or buy shoes for your kids, the cost is too high. The financial anxiety you might bring on yourself could be crippling. It's important to minimize the cost of failure for the good of your health, wealth and happiness. When we started Fanbytes, we purposefully paid ourselves only a small amount of money for the first year. We didn't want to get too used to a more comfortable income, because that would have increased the cost of failure.

Inexperience is a superpower because if you're young and inexperienced, the rhetoric of burning the boats doesn't really apply. There are no boats because there are no commitments. When I started Tim's Tutors, the only real cost of failure was that I might have lost my bet with Kunal and failed to earn £500 by the time I was 18. My livelihood did not depend on the scheme. Nobody was relying on me to put food on the table. In the context of entrepreneurship this was a good thing, because . . .

Every first business should fail

Every second business too. And probably every third. I guarantee that if you ask any successful entrepreneur about their journey, they will all have their war stories about businesses that failed, and from whose failure they learned more than they ever learned from success.

Inexperienced people are allowed to fail. In fact, inexperienced people are *expected* to fail. If a ten-year-old's lemonade stall loses money, nobody cares. It's part of the normal course of events. Inexperience is a superpower precisely because failure is an inevitable stepping stone on the path to success. It gives you the ammo you need to eventually be successful.

My tutoring business failed after a couple of months. My tutors were smart kids. It didn't take them long to work out that once I'd introduced them to a client, I no longer needed to be part of the transaction. They could pocket the full £15. As soon as that particular penny had dropped, Tim's Tutors was out of business. The failure of that tiny schoolboy enterprise taught me a great deal, both about myself and about the practicalities of entrepreneurship. I learned that I was the kind of person who had the get-up-and-go to build a business. I learned something about how money worked, and that it was possible to make money out of being a middleman. I learned that I needed to be online if I wanted to control the payment infrastructure and ensure that all the traffic had to go through me.

There were many other failures along the way. Here are a couple of examples.

My company Bandzie was a rip-off of an American company called Prizeo. It took the charity auction model and put it online. The idea was that you could buy charity merchandise from your favourite music artists or actors, and then be put into a competition to win an insanely great experience with said artist or actor. It failed for several reasons. Firstly, the culture in the UK was very different to the culture in the US. Over the pond, celebrities were far more inclined to engage with the concept. Secondly, we had no real access to the celebrities, whereas Prizeo had a co-founder who was already plugged in to the Hollywood scene. Thirdly, and most importantly, we were not solving a market need. We were simply taking a model that seemed to be successful elsewhere, and hoping it would travel. It didn't. So Bandzie failed, but that was OK, because we were young, the stakes were low and we learned from our mistakes.

The concept of Doodlr was similar to the concept of a company called Teespring, a site where a user could upload a design for a T-shirt or a mug and sell it online. A lot of people had made a lot of money on Teespring, so we knew the concept worked. Our version failed because we just weren't yet any good at entrepreneurship, and we couldn't quite figure out how to land customers. I'm sure that if I was starting that company now, I'd be much more successful. I'd focus on a niche where people were already fanatical – Harry Potter, or *Lord of the Rings*, or even a religious community – and I'd encourage them to upload their designs, with the offer of a prize to the person who sells the most. It would soon take off. Back then, however, I didn't understand sales and marketing, and so I had no hope of making a success of it. So Doodlr failed, but that was OK, because again the stakes were low and we learned from our mistakes.

YOUR INEXPERIENCE IS A SUPERPOWER

If I had first tried to start Fanbytes instead of Bandzie or Doodlr, I would have been clueless and it would have failed. The reason it was a success was because I'd got all my failures out of the way when I was young and it didn't matter.

> Forget the obsession with getting things right.
> Focus on getting them less wrong.
> One thing for certain is the first few times won't be good.
> Might as well get it over with.

Youth is a sandbox

When I was a little boy, I wanted to be a magician. Then I wanted to be a journalist. Then I wanted to be a behavioural economist (yes, really). In my childlike way, I tried being all these things for a few weeks, or sometimes months. I soon learned that I didn't want to be a magician *or* a journalist *or* a behavioural economist.

Youth is a superpower because when you're young, you can constantly reinvent who you are and what you want. You have several shots not just to decide what you love but more importantly to decide what you *don't* love and strike them off the list. In the sandbox of youth, the impact of following a path that turns out to be a dead end is almost zero. When it turned out I didn't want to be a magician after all, no tears were shed. When it turned out that Tim's Tutors was fatally flawed as a concept, I was frustrated for a couple of weeks, but it made no appreciable difference to my life. As a young entrepreneur, I was able to try lots of different ideas and allow my youthful exuberance to shrug off the frequent failures. The older you get, the greater the impact of those failures. There's no doubt that if Fanbytes had failed after four years of work, I'd have been a lot more distressed than I was about Tim's Tutors.

When you're young, you can experiment and follow your curiosity with no expectation that it should lead anywhere. This is a powerful freedom, so much so that certain companies encourage their employees to mimic the sandbox of youth. Google, for example, offer '20 per cent time', where 20 per cent of their employees' paid time is devoted to following their own muse. It turns out that this potentially aimless time, far from being wasted, becomes massively productive for the company as well as the individuals. There is value to following your nose wherever it may lead.

> As you get older, why not mimic the freedom of youth by creating a sandbox for experimentation. Perhaps you could schedule time in your calendar specifically to satisfy your curiosity. You could even follow Google's lead and award yourself 20 per cent time (or ten, or five) to follow your muse without the onus of expectation to produce something.

You can work hard

Entrepreneur Express came about because I loved business, I was constantly reading about business, and I thought: I wonder if there's a business to be made out of my love of business! I was editor of the school magazine at the time, and it became clear to me that publications such as *Business Insider* and *Forbes* were no more than that: publications about business. If someone else could do it, I could too. There was admirable naivety there, because without that thought I'd never have got started. The truth, though, is that editor-in-chief of *Forbes* is a big job. It's not something you can easily do alongside your A-levels, as I soon found out. I remember one weekend when I genuinely thought I was going to die from exhaustion. I was crouched over a laptop, writing till my fingers hurt, trying to work out distribution and marketing, doing everything required to launch a successful magazine all by myself.

I barely slept. For a while, I was a walking zombie. It didn't matter. Youth is a superpower because your capacity for crazy-hard work is so much greater. Youth lends you an almost inexhaustible supply of energy, or at least a supply that is easily replenished. And with no other commitments, the impact of your single-mindedness on others is minimal. If you burn yourself out when you're young, the wider implications are not so great.

People want to help

Youth may be a superpower, but that doesn't mean the wisdom of experience has no value. When I founded Fanbytes, I surrounded myself as far as possible (and as far as I could afford) with older, wiser employees. Now I encourage young entrepreneurs to seek mentoring from those who have been a few times around the block.

This is easier than you might imagine. Maybe it's out of altruism, maybe it's ego, maybe it's simply because older people see something of themselves in the young. Whatever the reason, many older people are inclined to help those younger than themselves. Inexperience is a superpower because it allows you to take advantage of this fact of human nature. Allow yourself to be mentored by those who have more experience than you. Be a sponge.

Some business ideas that harness your inexperience

When you're young and inexperienced, you have limited funds but almost unlimited time and energy. I'd like to give you three practical ideas that someone in that situation might use to earn a few thousand pounds here and there. These business ideas will not only provide an income. They'll teach you something about the entrepreneurial space, how business works and how wealthy people think.

Idea 1: A personal concierge service

As I write these words, I've recently scratched my car. It needs dealing with: a small job, but time-consuming.

A new door needs to be sourced. The door needs to be delivered to the body shop. The car needs to be delivered to the body shop. Then it needs to be delivered back to me. These are small administrative tasks that eat into my busy schedule and so cost me money. They take up time that has more value to me if I can focus it elsewhere. If someone approached me and offered to be on call to take these tasks off my plate for a few hundred pounds a month, they'd have a deal.

Personal concierge services exist, but a person with an abundance of time and energy, and few financial or personal commitments, can easily undercut these services. They'd be of great value to the cash-rich but time-poor. There's no shortage of these people. All you have to do is find them and make the approach. You'll soon have a viable business on your hands.

Idea 2: Trend research

Many experienced entrepreneurs struggle to find new trends, ideas and themes into which they might invest. Market-research firms exist to fill this gap, but they are very expensive and they don't really offer anything that a bright, young, independent researcher might offer, if they had time to spare and an enquiring mind. I'd give you some parameters – I might, for example, be interested in middleman businesses where the average contract price is £10,000. Your job would be the time-consuming legwork of sending me weekly lists of such companies, contact details of their CEOs and reasons why you think they might be worth investing in. If an investor could pay you £1,000 to do this rather than £10,000 to a company, it's a no-brainer – especially if you can introduce the investor to business spheres that are on your radar because of your youth, which might not be on his or her radar because of their age. You earn some cash, and you also learn something about how investors approach their business. Win-win.

Idea 3: Sell unused and unwanted items

People are forever getting rid of, for example, unwanted furniture. They sell it for very little on Facebook Marketplace and eBay, or even give it away for nothing on services such as Freecycle. With a bit of hustle and energy, you can collect these items, maybe spruce them up a little, and sell them on for perhaps even a margin of 100 per cent. You might need a car, but otherwise your start-up costs are next to nothing, and the size of your business is limited only by your energy and enthusiasm.

The basic ideas behind these three suggestions are to help rich people make their lives easier, to identify a service that's expensive when a company does it but cheap when an individual does it, and to make good use of waste products. These ideas can of course be used to come up with all sorts of other hustles. All you need is the time and energy to do it. If you're young, you have it. Another reason why your inexperience is a superpower.

The most important lesson an inexperienced person can learn

Starting young helps you with business skills, for sure. You learn what works and – perhaps more importantly – what doesn't. Starting young helps you with mental skills, too, such as creativity and resilience. There is one key mental skill that is much more easily learned when you're still levelling up your experience. It's a skill that you can hone with the three ideas above, and it is this: the confidence and chutzpah to ask strangers for money.

Most people never have to do this. The average person in the average job on the average salary is given an amount of money that has already been decided by someone else. You only have to think about the anxiety people generally feel when they want to ask for a pay rise to realize that asking for money is a skill very few of us have, and a process many of us would rather avoid. If you want to be an entrepreneur or make it in business, this mindset isn't going to work for you. At its heart, business is nothing more than coming up with a solution to a problem and asking someone to pay you to solve that problem. You'd better get used to asking strangers for money. Inexperience is a superpower because this is much more easily done on a small scale when you're younger. I can draw a straight line between the young Timothy Armoo asking his schoolmates to pay him £10 for a tutoring session, to the older Timothy Armoo asking complete strangers to invest half a million pounds in his company. My ability to make the larger request was borne of my ability to make the smaller one. Could I have done it without the other? Maybe, but it would have been a damn sight harder.

Harness the superpower of inexperience when you're older

Perhaps, having read this chapter, you're thinking it's game over for entrepreneurs who are no longer in the full flush of youth. Not a bit of it. Inexperience is a superpower when we're young, but it's a superpower when we're older too, so long as we're prepared to challenge the received wisdom that the inexperience of youth is a hindrance, and take steps to recapture its naivety and enthusiasm.

Often, when people have never done something before, they see it as a negative. I disagree. We started this chapter talking about the naivety of youth. I believe that inexperience in a particular field gives us the opportunity to recapture some of that naivety and to approach problems from first principles. There were many times during the Fanbytes journey that social-media platforms changed or algorithms altered. Each time it happened, we found ourselves presented with the barrier of our own inexperience, but this was not a bad thing. It forced us to think originally. It forced me to become that 14-year-old boy again, trying to work out how to source a biology tutor and taking the simplest, most naive path.

YOUR INEXPERIENCE IS A SUPERPOWER

As we've seen, when you're young you have the time to indulge your interests and your hobbies before the considerable commitments of work and family kicks in. Even in later life, however, I believe we can harness the superpower of inexperience by trying to remember that youth-like curiosity and making room for it. I find that as I grow older, I feel more trepidation about how I choose to spend my time. It can be a hindrance. The solution is to try to recapture your youthful enthusiasm. To work on a project because you love it, rather than for any more mundane financial imperative. There's a reason some companies curate their environment with bean bags and table tennis tables and free smoothies. By cultivating a fun environment and harnessing our youthful longing for play and enjoyment, we become more creative and more effective.

So, if you're no longer young, cultivate a similar environment for yourself, one that recalls what was important to you when you *were* young. Surround yourself with fun people. Allow yourself a little wide-eyed enthusiasm. These are all attributes of youth, but they can be the attributes of later life too, if you'll only let them. And if you can merge the naivety of expectation with the benefits of experience, you'll have potent tools with which to do business.

The Cheat Sheet

- The naive approach can often be the best. Don't complicate matters.
- Young people know things older people don't. They're plugged into a different part of the culture. That gives them an advantage and makes them valuable.
- Young people have the time, opportunity and resilience to fail. Failure is an essential stepping stone on the path to success.
- Young people have space to work out what they enjoy, and more importantly what they don't.
- The advantages of youthful inexperience can be harnessed even when you're older.

Cheatcode 3:
Make It Easy To Win

Growing up, I used to think life had to be hard.

Partly, that was because life *was* hard for the people around me living on a rough council estate in south London. There wasn't much money to go around. There was poverty and there was violence. When my friend Kunal bet me that I'd never have £500 in my pocket before the age of 18, it was a pretty safe bet. To most people, it would have seemed too hard.

All this, however, was massively accentuated by the diet of 'motivational' YouTube videos I fed myself in my desire to become a successful entrepreneur.

I bet you know the type of thing. Badass, high-achieving dudes, shouting at you that you're WEAK if you don't put in the work. That you're AFRAID of the effort. That you're LESS OF A PERSON if you don't walk through fire to achieve your goals. And if you don't know that kind of thing? Search for motivational videos and you'll soon see what I mean.

Now, perhaps these videos will have the desired effect and motivate you to embrace the hardship of life. Perhaps they'll have the opposite effect and demotivate you entirely. As a teenager and in my early twenties, I used those videos for motivation. I bought into it. I believed the message that success was entirely a function of how hard you were prepared to grind. How much pain you were prepared to put yourself through. Those YouTube motivational gurus were like testosterone-fuelled guys in the gym, getting all pumped up with each other before they can smash their PBs at the bench press. They chose the hard way. NO PAIN, NO GAIN!

But here's the thing. When I started going to the gym myself, I discovered that the chest-beating, gym-bro persona was not what worked best for me. Instead, I found the opposite: that if I cut myself some slack, treated the whole endeavour like fun and thought of ways to make the process of getting in shape easier, my motivation increased and my results hit the fast track.

What's true in the gym is true in business and in life. It doesn't have to be hard, at least not all the time. We don't have to buy into the fallacy that the perpetual hustle-grind is the only route to success. I'm not suggesting that we should dismiss the notion of hard work or fail to take our life and our business seriously. I'm suggesting that we alter our expectations: if we *expect* things to be very hard, we'll end up *treating* them as very hard, which means they'll end up *being* very hard.

Instead, we should apply one of our most important cheatcodes and make it easy to win.

Make it fun

I was watching two guys contest the high jump during the Olympics. They were both trying to clear a particular bar and it was obviously very difficult. Mentality is an important component of any sporting event, of course, and one of the contestants was doing everything he could to get the crowd on his side. He'd turn to them and get them all jazzed up, encouraging them to cheer and inject some motivational spirit into the atmosphere. It made sense: I could see what he was doing and why he was doing it. Like the gym bros, he was trying to energize himself and gain those few extra per cent.

Except . . . he kept hitting the bar. His strategy wasn't working.

Then, on one occasion, he jumped, hit the bar and started to laugh a bit. Something in his demeanour changed. He seemed less tense, less concerned about the crowd. Now, you could write what I know about the high jump on the back of a postage stamp, but as I watched him prepare for his next attempt, I thought to myself: he's going to clear it. I could just tell.

And he did.

Sometimes, we face a big moment. We think to ourselves: this is the one. This really matters. Our body goes into angst mode. We don't feel as free and lucid as we might. Like the high jumper, we make our job more difficult by over-emphasizing its seriousness. If we can find a way of injecting a bit of fun, we alter our expectations. If we can capture a sense of playfulness, we stop ourselves from making things harder than we need to.

Note that I'm not saying we shouldn't take life seriously, or that we shouldn't put in effort. I'm saying that if we alter our presumption of difficulty, we remove a mental barrier for ourselves.

Which leads me to a controversial opinion . . .

A controversial opinion

As a Black entrepreneur, I'm constantly presented with the received wisdom that entrepreneurship is an order of magnitude harder for Black people than it is for others. The statistics, I'm told, reflect this difficulty, because only a tiny percentage of Black entrepreneurs receive funding. It's empirically the case, so the narrative goes, that it's tougher for us. The cards are not stacked in our favour.

I'm afraid I don't have much time for this perspective. Now and then, this has landed me in trouble. I've been accused of denouncing my Blackness, whatever that means. But I stick by my opinion. If I go into the game thinking, Ah man, it's so hard to be a Black entrepreneur, I'm automatically going to expect it to be very hard to raise money. If I tell myself that an investor won't invest in me because I'm Black, and I believe the story I tell myself that I'm already on the back foot, then guess what: I probably won't be able to raise that money. If I expect something to be hard, I'll treat it as hard. If I allow myself to succumb to a narrative of overwhelming difficulty, I make it harder to win, not easier.

So here's an alternative perspective: being a Black

entrepreneur is a massive competitive advantage. I truly believe this. Being in a minority, I stand out. There are loads of organizations that provide grants and support programmes for Black entrepreneurs, which means I have access to a set of resources that many other people don't. In certain environments, minorities are easily underestimated, which makes it easier to outperform expectations.

You may not be a Black entrepreneur, but you may believe that there are hurdles unique to your situation or demographic that negatively affect your chances of success. And they will, if you let them. If, however, you are able to reset your assumptions, you make it vastly easier to win. Our expectations matter.

> Never victimize yourself.
> If you do, no one will care.
> But your growth will stop.
> So the only person who loses is you.

MAKE IT EASY TO WIN

Recalibrate your expectations

Let's go back to the gym. When I was an admittedly slightly chubby 22-year-old, I decided that the time had come to get into shape. I thought to myself: what do people do when they want to get into shape? What are their inputs? Well, they generally eat a bit less food, they prioritize protein and they go to the gym. So I decided I'd do that. Simple.

Except, of course, it's not that simple. At least, it's not that simple if we've taken the decision not to follow the no-pain-no-gain, you're-weak-if-you-don't-work approach of those YouTube videos that formed my thinking when I was a younger man. Because let's face it: sometimes we get distracted. Sometimes we get demotivated. Sometimes I'm going to go out for dinner and the food's so good I'll order seconds. Sometimes I'll get dessert. Sometimes I'll really – *really* – not want to go to the gym. So what am I going to do? It seems to me I have two options. I could berate myself for my lack of motivation and self-control, and resign myself to this being the beginning of a downward spiral. Alternatively, I could calmly say, 'OK, I'm going to eat dessert and not go to the gym. But tomorrow I'll get myself back on track.'

I can acknowledge that sometimes the gym will be boring and mitigate against that likely eventuality by taking a friend. I can predict that there will be bumps in the road.

This mindset is crucial in the world of business. In the early days of Fanbytes, I'd worked out that it was quite an obvious business to grow, scale and sell. I didn't think it would be an insanely hard project because I knew other people were doing something similar. Equally, however, I knew it wouldn't be completely easy. I considered the potential difficulties. Algorithms would change. Social-media platforms would come and go. Competitors would enter the same space. Some people would undercut us on price. I made an active decision to set my expectations, and so, when things went wrong, it wasn't a complete surprise. It didn't put us off course.

We make it easier to win when we recalibrate our expectations about how the future will unfold, acknowledging that there will be difficulties and giving ourselves permission not to be anxious or scared about that outcome. If we expect no complications, we'll be disappointed. If we prepare for unexpected hitches, we're less likely to be derailed when they occur.

Normalizing success

One of my favourite books is *Psycho-Cybernetics* by Dr Maxwell Maltz. It was first published in 1960 and introduced its readers to the psychology of self-image and how it impacts our success and happiness. A plastic surgeon by profession, Maltz made the observation that after a physical transformation, some people experienced an uptick in their self-esteem while others didn't; they continued to consider themselves 'flawed' in some way. He drew the conclusion that our self-image is often more powerful than reality. We find it difficult to tell the difference between what is real and what is imagined.

In Maltz's view, the patient whose scar has been healed through plastic surgery and who still believes themselves to be flawed has essentially brainwashed themselves into a fixed perception of the sort of person they are. Similarly, the salesman who cannot break the 50k sales target even when he's placed in an environment where everyone else is routinely breaking the 500k sales target: this person has defined themselves as a 50k person and cannot break out of that way of thinking. They've told themselves this story so many times, they now act as if it's a fact.

It's not a fact, and one of Maltz's great insights is

that we can harness this tendency to reshape our self-perception. Our first cheatcode was We Are The Stories We Tell Ourselves. In that chapter, I told you how, as a very young man, I would put on my smartest clothes and go to work in the foyer of Claridge's. My aim was to normalize the idea of success in my mind, to take advantage of the fact that the brain finds it difficult to tell the difference between what is real and what is imagined, and to reprogramme the image I had of myself.

I did this in other ways too as I grew older, most notably by placing myself in environments where I was the least smart and the least successful. I would attend networking events with entrepreneurs who had raised tens of millions of pounds – sums that completely dwarfed the money I had managed to raise. I went to private equity discussions where I had no clue what anybody was talking about. I'd have to go home to research the words and concepts. This was an uncomfortable process. I'd feel small. My ego took a bit of a bash. But by putting myself in those situations, I normalized the idea that I deserved to be there. I gave myself permission to think on a much grander scale than I would have done if I'd simply stayed within my comfort zone.

Making it easy to win is not about making it easy all the time. Reprogramming our self-image can be a bruising process, because it forces us to admit that we're not where we want to be. But the hard path now leads to the easy path later: you can make it inevitable that you will win by changing your circumstances and normalizing a future version of yourself.

Have a small, deep group of winners

In the same way that we can make it easy to win by adapting our surroundings in a way that normalizes success, so we can make a conscious effort to surround ourselves with people whose presence in our lives has an inevitably positive impact on us. For me, this means focusing my attention on a small, deep group of six to eight people who are significantly better than me at doing certain things, rather than devoting too much of my time to a larger, broader group.

The people in my small, deep group need not be in the same business as me. They do their thing, I do my thing. Their presence in my life, however, means that almost by osmosis I derive many benefits that make it easier for me to succeed in my own endeavours. I learn from their expertise and experience. I receive valuable feedback and constructive criticism from people whose opinion I trust and respect. I reap the benefit of their diverse perspectives to broaden my own. Their presence in my life means I'm more inclined to hold myself to a higher standard.

In the first instance, this process of curating a small, deep group of peers can be just as ego-bruising as the process of placing yourself in an environment where you're the least smart and least successful. But in both these scenarios we make it easy to win by enduring the initial pain of feeling a little inferior.

That initial feeling of inferiority soon pays dividends, and it does so almost inevitably. In his book *Atomic Habits*, James Clear proposed that 'You do not rise to the level of your goals, you fall to the level of your systems.' I think that this is a very profound observation. It implies that the level of our success is a function of the processes we put in place rather than a desire to achieve certain objectives. We fall to the default level of the systems we create for ourselves. If those systems comprise the influence of a consciously selected group of smart, highly capable, ambitious people, then our default level is going to be that of a smart, highly capable, ambitious person. It happens almost automatically.

MAKE IT EASY TO WIN

The path of least resistance

I have been diagnosed with ADHD. A feature of this particular neurodivergent condition is that it accentuates my tendency to procrastinate. I'll know a long time in advance that I have to do a particular thing, but I won't prepare for it until the very last minute. I once had to talk at a big marketing conference. The conference took place the day after my cousin's wedding. I'd known about my commitment six weeks in advance, but predictably enough I was still editing the slides on the train back from the wedding. It meant I ran out of time to send the slides to the organizers to load on the system. I plugged my laptop into their projector in front of more than a thousand delegates and – you guessed it – it broke down. Talk about my procrastination coming back to bite me.

You don't need to be neurodiverse for procrastination to be an issue. I think this is something a lot of people suffer from, and the reason is that when a big job looms, we find it hard to get started. Even smaller jobs can build up in our minds, developing into bigger obstacles than they need to be. We can make it easier to win by finding a way to get started on projects that we've been putting off, so that we can build momentum. For me, that means following the path of least resistance.

When we follow the path of least resistance, we observe a natural tendency to follow a route to an end goal that avoids obstacles and difficulty. Like water and electricity, humans generally prefer to avoid resistance and opt for shortcuts. Following the path of least resistance can have negative outcomes. In our decision-making processes we often try to avoid cognitive strain by relying on familiar, well-worn solutions to the exclusion of potentially more effective alternatives. In our personal relationships, we often avoid discussing difficult or emotive topics, choosing instead to default to subjects that we know will not cause upset or offence. This can lead us to avoid dealing with underlying problems or unspoken resentments.

So, following the path of least resistance is not always a good thing. It can be a cop-out. There are, however, in my opinion, ways in which we can use this technique to increase our chances of overcoming obstacles. Sometimes, following the path of least resistance can make it easier to win. This is particularly the case if, like me, you are prone to procrastination.

Let me give you an example that happened on the very day I wrote these pages. Every day, I aim to perform certain mobility exercises, in order that I remain as flexible as possible. I know that these are good for me. I know that doing them is all upside and no downside. I *want* to do them. But sometimes I put them off. I procrastinate. One particular exercise involves lying on your back on the floor and raising your knee to strengthen your hamstring. Nothing more complicated or energetic than that but this morning, as I lay in bed, I couldn't be bothered. It just felt like too big a deal. (Did someone say ADHD?) I felt bad about my inability to start, so instead I followed the path of least resistance. I lay under my duvet and did a couple of reps. You're not supposed to do the exercise on a soft surface like a mattress, but that didn't matter. As soon as I'd done the first three or four reps, I felt a bit more alive. I rolled down on to the floor and started doing the exercise properly.

If I hadn't found the path of least resistance, an easy way to get going, another day would have passed without me doing the exercise. There is power in starting.

I have found that this translates into my wider life, and certainly into business. I knew for a long time, while we were running Fanbytes, that we needed a new sales deck (the presentation we used to pitch our services). Our offering had become much more mature, and this was not represented in our old deck. I knew this meant that we were missing sales. A new sales deck would directly result in more sales, which would directly result in more income, which would directly benefit me. I could not have had more of a vested interest in creating that new sales deck.

And yet, I procrastinated. A month went by. Two months. Three. I put it off. Why? Because creating a new sales deck is a lot of effort. You have to think about the structure, you have to find the right case studies, you have to educate the team about it . . . It all requires a high degree of cognitive strain. But this was getting ridiculous. The upsides of doing it were so vast. So one day I thought to myself: what is the path of least resistance? What is the smallest thing I can do to just start? I sat down and typed a few rough bullet points on my phone. They weren't perfect. They weren't even particularly good. But they were a start, and they meant I'd done the first bit. Just as when I raised my leg while lying on the mattress, they gave me a little bump of momentum. I went on to create two slides. Then four. Within a week, I'd done it. This job had taken months to get started, and I'd managed to complete it by forcing myself to do the smallest possible thing: typing out some junk on my phone.

Compounding is a powerful process. Small, incremental actions, when repeated, lead to major progress.

MAKE IT EASY TO WIN

Sometimes the path of least resistance makes it easy to win because it's the direct route to where you want to be.

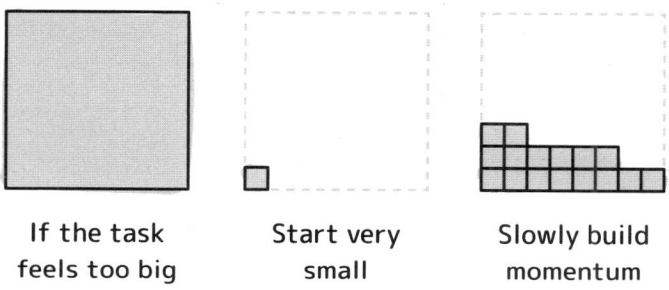

| If the task feels too big | Start very small | Slowly build momentum |

Rules are your friend

Steve Jobs famously wore the same clothes every day: black turtleneck, blue jeans and sneakers. He did this, in part, to relieve decision fatigue. By reducing the number of trivial decisions he had to make in a day, he freed up his headspace for more important decisions. I tried following his lead in wearing a personal uniform, but it turns out I like wearing nice – and different – clothes too much! The principle behind Jobs's strategy is sound, however. Decision fatigue is real. We make it easy to win by eliminating the number of conscious decisions we have to make. In order to do this, rules are our friend.

Here's a rule I live by: no snacking. I eat three meals

a day – breakfast, lunch and dinner – and nothing in between. Applying that rule to my life helps me stick to a good habit. It's a simple example of how we can intentionally design our life in such a way that our desired behaviour becomes our default behaviour. It's a question of reducing friction by automating our decision-making process and reducing the need for willpower. It's also a question of creating safeguards so that the busyness of life doesn't lead us to ignore or devalue important aspects of it. Our rules don't need to be punitive or restrictive. We can ensure that we maintain the health of our romantic relationships by ring-fencing a date night once a week. If we're parents of young children, we can insist on dedicated time spent playing with them. These rules are easy ways of nurturing good habits and encouraging positive outcomes.

Imposing rules on ourselves in a business setting makes it easy to win because it promotes consistency and efficiency. For me, this largely centres on time-management. If I know that every Monday between 9am and 10am I'm going to check our sales targets, and every Wednesday at midday I'm going to sit down with my finance team to look at the numbers, it means that I don't have to think about scheduling these activities or risk ignoring them because I don't have the necessary systems in place. It frees me up to concentrate on those activities and decisions that actually move the needle.

Earlier in this chapter, we referenced James Clear's notion that we do not rise to the level or our goals, we fall to the level of our systems. Acknowledging that rules are our friends is a way of harnessing this observation by putting in place rigorous, helpful systems that limit our very human tendency to err towards procrastination and inefficiency.

> How to get things done: use the 'rule of 3'.
> Three 90-minute blocks of deep work.
> Three objectives for the month.
> Three critical tasks for the day.
> Easy to remember.
> Easy to manage.
> Easy to execute.
> Block out all the noise.
> Go all in.

'Through discipline comes freedom.'
attr. Aristotle

The 80/20 rule

The 80/20 rule is the notion that 20 per cent of our inputs account for 80 per cent of our outputs. It's not a rigid mathematical law, of course. It's a useful heuristic that helps us concentrate on the efficiency of our inputs. I've observed it to be true both in business and in general life.

At the beginning of Fanbytes, our attention was all over the place. We were obsessed with the newness of things. We constantly wanted to introduce new products and services because that's what we thought the market required. We would devote many hours to these endeavours, and we thought we were doing the right thing because we saw that a lot of our competitors in the industry were acting similarly. The trouble was, of all the many services we found ourselves offering, only two were profitable: the influencer service and the content-creation service. The rest were a time-and-resource suck for no appreciable benefit.

I had to sit down and make a decision. In order to achieve our end goal of building a business that could be scaled and sold, what did we need to concentrate on? The answer was: profitability and client retention. If we properly managed those two aspects of the business, happy days.

And so we cut out the fat. Having observed that a large percentage of our outputs originated from a small percentage of our inputs, we streamlined our efforts. It made it easier to reach our endgame.

This approach is particularly applicable to marketing. Of all the marketing channels that we employed to promote the business, only two worked, which were Google Ads and content marketing. Everything else – speaking engagements, Facebook affiliates – turned out to be a waste of time for us. Indeed, the rule is applicable to so many aspects of life, not least in our personal relationships, where a small proportion of our connections are responsible for a large proportion of our wellbeing. We make it easy to win when we recognize this fact, and make arrangements to our lives accordingly.

> *'It's not the daily increase but the daily decrease, hack away the unessential.'*
> *Bruce Lee*

Keep your identity small

The ability to pivot is crucial to entrepreneurs. Fanbytes was an iteration of a previous idea, and this is commonplace in the world of business. Netflix started out as a DVD rental-by-mail service before Reed Hastings recognized the potential of digital streaming. Slack was merely a component of a failed online game before its developers recognized its value as a communication tool. Entrepreneurs who stick too rigidly to their original ideas make it much harder to win by limiting their ability to adapt to changing circumstances.

Adaptability is crucial outside of business, too. And it's hard. As humans, we have a tendency to label ourselves, and to link our identities to those labels. We might say to ourselves 'I am a dietician' or 'I am an actor' or 'I am an accountant.' The more we stick to these labels, the more our identities become fixed. They take us over, and this can make it harder to win because it restricts our options. Lives, and careers, are not a straight shot. They meander. From time to time, like entrepreneurs, we're going to need to pivot. To change direction. To be fleet of foot and able to alter our trajectory. If we have a fixed sense of our own identities, this is much harder to do. It becomes difficult – painful even – to change our perception of who we think we are. This holds us back.

If we can keep our identity small, however, we limit our tendency to become tied to a particular label and make it easier to try something new. That's why, if I must apply a label to myself, I think of myself as a 'learner' rather than something more specific and therefore limiting.

Live like a lion

Some people say you should be always 'on'. Like the motivational gurus on YouTube on whose every word I used to hang as a younger man, they see downtime as weakness. If you're going to be a winner, according to this view of the world, you'd better make sure you bring your A-game to every minute of the hour and every hour of the day.

I don't think this makes it easier to win at all. It's unsustainable, it's exhausting and it's not much fun. It's also massively inefficient. If you're expending your emotional and physical energy when you require it least, you risk lacking that energy when it's most needed.

It's far better, in my opinion, to live like a lion.

Lions spend a large proportion of their time just . . . chillin'! For them, hunting is a high-energy activity and it's important that they conserve that energy for the moment when it's required. We can learn from that. Success isn't about constant intensity. There are times when you'll need to step things up and when balance won't exist for you. When those moments come, you pounce. You go all in and you do whatever needs to be done. How long those bursts of intensity last depends on the circumstances. It could be weeks, months or even years. But just as it's important to match the intensity when the time comes, so it's important to enjoy the periods of calm.

When it's time to hunt, you hunt. When it's time to chill, you chill.

Do the easy stuff well

Finally, the most effective way to make it easy to win is – unsurprisingly – the easiest. Do the easy stuff well!

You'll often hear sports managers talk about the importance of nailing the basics. You become a hard team to beat if the fundamentals of your performance are solid. What's true in sport is true in life. Turn up on time. Look smart (when customer-facing companies insist that their employees dress well, it improves company performance). These are tiny hacks that give you a massive advantage over the surprisingly large number of people who ignore them. They don't just encourage people to treat you more seriously. By activating them, you send yourself a signal: I am the sort of person who can get the basics done.

Above all, address others properly. I receive hundreds of messages every week from enterprising people. So many of them don't nail the simple task of communicating in a professional manner. A good example of this, in my world, is the constant use of the word 'bro'. I hate this. It's meant to be familiar, but it presents you as young, unprofessional and unserious. Your potential employer is not your bro. Your potential customer is not your bro. Your potential investor is not your bro. When you use this kind of language, you're self-sabotaging and – probably without even knowing it – excluding yourself from the conversation.

Make sure you're punctual and smart. Don't be distracted in meetings or look at your phone when you're supposed to be interacting with a colleague. Do what you say you're going to do. Be reliable. The sort of person who applies these easy fixes to their life makes it much, much easier to win.

The Cheat Sheet

- Don't believe the motivational gurus who tell you that life *has* to be hard. It doesn't.
- When we inject a bit of fun, we alter our presumption of difficulty and remove a mental barrier.
- When we expect there to be bumps in the road, we make it easier to deal with problems when they arise.
- A small, deep group of peers will raise your default level.
- Rules make decisions easier by automating the trivial stuff.
- At some point we all have to pivot. We make it easier to do this by keeping our identity small.
- When it's time to hunt, you hunt. When it's time to chill, you chill!

Cheatcode 4: Do It Scared

Ring, ring. Ring, ring.

'Hello, Timo,' says a voice.

'Hi!' I squeak.

It's 9am on a Wednesday morning. My first video call of the day. And it's a big one, because for the first time ever I'm going to ask a potential client to pay us £10,000.

I'm scared.

Like, *really* scared.

I've asked for money before, of course. Ever since the days of Tim's Tutors I've been plucking up the courage to charge people for my services, and my previous business sold for way more than ten grand. But somehow, this is different. Fanbytes is in its infancy. So is the whole notion of influencer marketing. We're uncertain of our value. We've only completed two campaigns – for an outdoor activity company and a clothing store – and for those campaigns we've been significantly underpricing ourselves. We charged £300 for one campaign and £700 for the other. For that money we offered one influencer and 50,000 views on YouTube. A good deal for the brands, not so much for us. We have to up our game. So our strategy for this new client – a posh popcorn brand – is to ask for £10,000 for three influencers to drum up 30,000 views. Over ten times the money for half the service. Even though our original pricing was ridiculously low and we should never have done it, this feels like a big leap. It feels like we might get found out. It feels like we might get laughed out of town.

Which is why I'm scared.

So scared, in fact, that I can't look my client in the eye. I open up a separate tab on my computer so I don't have to see my client's face. Much easier that way. Much less scary.

Deep breath. Build up to the money. 'I think your brand would probably be a good fit for an influencer marketing campaign,' I say.

'I agree. That's why I'm on the call.'

'Great. So, we've identified that the core audience for this campaign would be students, and we'd like to suggest three particular influencers who we think will fit that audience.'

'Why do you think that?'

'Their demographics show that they have a good

proportion of the student audience. They understand them. They're really able to engage them.'

Silence. I don't know if she's pausing to think of a question or if there's a problem with the connection, or if she's just plain old unimpressed. I feel a bead of sweat drip down the nape of my neck. I continue to talk.

'A campaign might look like this: the influencer is studying, and needs to take a break, and talks about having your popcorn as a healthy snack . . .'

Again, silence.

I have to cut to the chase. I can't put it off any longer.

'With these three influencers, we'll guarantee you –' I gulp. 'Thirty thousand views.'

Silence.

'And for all this, the fee will be t—'

As I mentioned in chapter one, as a child I suffered from a fairly significant stutter. I've managed to overcome it, but when I'm anxious it still reappears.

'It'll be t—'

Deep breath. *Do it scared.*

'It'll be ten thousand pounds.'

Silence.

I feel sick. I've been found out.

And then she says: 'Yeah, OK.'

I blink. I smile. The anxiety melts away. It turns out I didn't need to be scared after all.

Or maybe I did. Because maybe doing it scared is an important skill.

It's a common misconception that people who achieve significant things aren't scared. That they feel no anxiety or apprehension before attempting something difficult or uncomfortable. We imagine that they have some kind of robotic ability to feel no fear. This misconception is exacerbated by social media: people can so easily curate versions of themselves that present a fearless, uber-confident demeanour that we're easily tricked into believing it's an accurate reflection of what's going on inside. It isn't. Apprehension and anxiety are completely normal, experienced by all right-thinking humans. The challenge lies both in not letting the fear hold you back, and crucially in harnessing it to improve your outcomes. In this chapter we're going to think about some ways of achieving that aim.

> Champions aren't fearless. They just do it scared.
> That same crazy, heavy feeling in the pit of your stomach, they had too.

> That same leg shake before you gave that presentation, they had too.
>
> That same restless uncertainty about taking the leap, they had too.
>
> But the difference is, they did it.

Your 'do it scared' muscle

That first time I asked for £10,000 for a campaign, I was terrified. And do you know what? The first time I charged £100,000 for a campaign was the same. The bead of sweat, the stutter, the unwillingness to look my potential client in the eye.

But here's the thing. The first time I asked for £200,000 for a campaign, I found it a little easier. Sure, I was about to ask for far more than I'd ever requested, but somehow I felt significantly less anxious about the proposition. The reason for this, I think, is because I'd been exercising my 'do it scared' muscle. Like any muscle, the more you use it, the stronger it becomes.

You could replay the same scenario for the first time I asked investors for money. Our first fundraising request was for £25,000. Man, I rehearsed that pitch to within

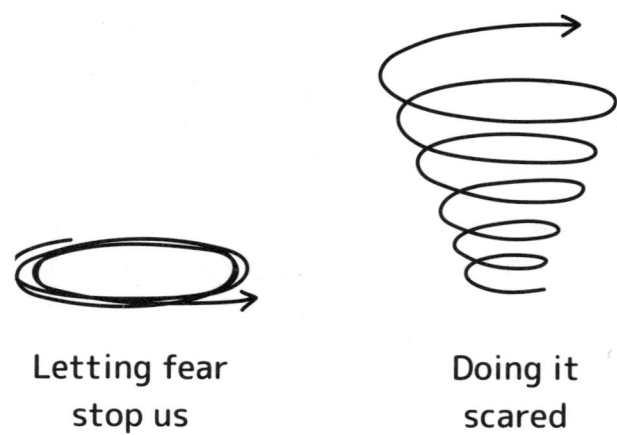

| Letting fear stop us | Doing it scared |

an inch of its life and I was terrified when presenting it. And when it came to asking for half a million? Same deal. Having exercised my 'do it scared' muscles in those two scenarios, however, the first time I asked for a million pounds was a much less stressful experience. Like a newbie in the gym working on their bicep curl, I'd broken through the discomfort that comes with exercising a new muscle.

Business, and life, routinely present us with new difficulties. The decision we have to make is whether to turn away from them, or engage with the strain. The more we engage with it, the less strenuous it becomes.

'Do the thing you fear and the death of fear is certain.'
attr. Ralph Waldo Emerson

I am not enough

When I look back on those early exchanges with the benefit of hindsight, I realize that I misinterpreted the reason for my fear. I used to think that it derived from a belief that I'm not enough. Other people were obviously better at these things than me and they were obviously not scared to attempt them. I now realize that this isn't true. Other people *aren't* better than me and the fear I felt derived from my attempt to do something new and unfamiliar. Just as we experience discomfort when we first start exercising a particular muscle group in our body, so it's perfectly natural to experience it when we exercise our 'do it scared' muscle.

Do not self-sabotage

Let me take you back to the first time I was offered a paid speaking engagement. I'd spoken in public before, and even managed to overcome my stutter and the natural anxiety many people experience when asked to speak in front of a crowd. To be paid, however, was a whole different ball game. The event was a marketing conference in Belfast. They offered to pay my travel and accommodation, and they wanted to know my fee.

The moment that email request landed in the inbox of my little red Toshiba laptop, I felt a knot in my stomach. My *fee*? What the heck? It had never occurred to me that anybody would actually want to pay money to hear what I had to say. I felt sheepish at the very idea of charging. They wanted a number, however, so I mustered the courage to ask for £800 and they immediately agreed. So the deal was done. I would fly to Belfast to perform the speaking engagement. Happy days.

The happy day arrived. So why did I not *feel* happy? Why did I feel scared? The moment came for me to leave for the airport. I faffed and hesitated and delayed. By the time I'd reached the check-in desk, my flight had left. I'd missed it. There was another flight to Belfast leaving imminently, however, so the organizers booked me on to that one and I was soon in the air.

I realize now, even if I didn't realize it at the time, that missing that flight was no accident. At some level, I missed that flight intentionally. I was scared of giving the talk, so a tiny part of my brain told me that if I missed the flight, I could reasonably present a narrative that excused me from the anxiety-inducing commitment:

'I wanted to do it – I really did – but here's the unfortunate thing: I missed my flight.'

I think this tendency to self-sabotage when we're scared of performing a task is common, albeit often subconscious. It's a means of avoiding the task, and it manifests in various ways. We might procrastinate, telling ourselves and others that we're not quite ready, that there's benefit in delaying, even though the real reason for the delay is fear. We might hide behind a shield of perfectionism, succumbing to our fear by holding ourselves and our endeavours to an unrealistic standard as a means of avoiding the endeavour itself. (Fun fact: you can perform worse than you prefer and still well enough to make progress. Consistency trumps perfectionism every time.)

It can be hard to mitigate against these moments of self-sabotage, precisely because they often happen subconsciously or present themselves as superficially tempting behaviours. That's why it's important to force yourself to be aware of the possibility of self-sabotage whenever you feel scared to tackle a particular problem. Carefully examine your motives. Are you being as rational as you pretend in delaying an uncomfortable task? Or are you just allowing yourself to give in to the fear?

> The body you want is in the training you avoid. The talent you want is the practice you avoid. The wealth you want is the uncertainties you avoid. The life you want is the challenges you avoid. Don't self-sabotage. Stop avoiding.

Set expectations

I can't swim. At least, not at the time of writing. Perhaps by the time you read these words, I'll have learned because I'm currently having lessons. My fear of water limits me, so I need to overcome it.

For the past few lessons, I've been learning to scull. This is when you move your hands in a figure of eight to keep yourself afloat. Between you and me, I'd been nailing it. But then, after some successful lessons, I climbed into the pool, tried to scull and couldn't get myself to float.

Now, not being able to float when you're a weak swimmer is a scary proposition, and I won't pretend that the moment didn't induce a little anxiety. However, it wasn't as scary as it might have been because before starting my swimming lessons, I set my expectations.

I told myself that my progress was likely to be erratic. Some days my lessons would go well, some days they wouldn't. So, when my sculling was not as brilliant as I'd hoped, my fear of the water was not compounded by an unexpected inability to float. I didn't feel particularly uncomfortable or embarrassed by it. I was able to say: 'Ah well, that sucks, but I knew it would happen at some point.' I was able to see it as part of the game.

This mental technique of setting your expectations is crucial in business and in life. We discussed it in the context of our previous cheatcode, Make It Easy To Win. It's just as relevant when dealing with our fears because by expecting that fear is part of the process, we diminish the impact of that fear. By anticipating complexity, we make life simpler.

Beware the comfort chamber

You'll have heard people talking about their comfort zone. It's the level at which we function easily and without any sense of cognitive or physical strain. Some people call it a comfort pit – a hole that you want to get out of as quickly as possible – but I'm not so sure about that. A hole is a grim place to live, whereas this place is superficially rather welcoming. I prefer to think of it as a comfort chamber.

It's a lovely place, our comfort chamber. There's a big, squashy sofa, there's a TV on the wall, there's all our favourite food and drink on tap. There's plenty of space and it's well insulated from the difficulties of the outside world. Make no mistake: our comfort chamber is a luxurious place to hang out.

The trouble is, our comfort chamber is really a prison. A pleasant, appealing prison for sure, but still a prison. It restricts us, because if we only ever do what's comfortable to us, we never truly grow. In order to do that, we have to open the door of the chamber and step outside. You'd better believe that it's going to be uncomfortable to do this, especially if you've been vibing in that chamber for any appreciable period of time. It's scary to step outside the comfort chamber, but I'm sure most people would agree that it's a good thing to do now and then.

We think of fear as a negative emotion, and sometimes, of course, it is. If that fear leads us to limit ourselves and to exclude new experiences from our lives, if it leads us down the path of self-sabotage, it's entirely to be avoided. Properly framed, however, and met head on, it's a good thing. It allows you to learn and grow. It increases your confidence by exercising your 'do it scared' muscle.

It opens up opportunities that are simply never available to you if you stay inside the cosy four walls of your comfort chamber.

Fight or flight

Imagine you're an international rugby player preparing to take the field, or a 100-metre sprinter about to go for gold. You've done this a hundred times before. You've worked, you've trained, you back yourself.

But somewhere, in a little part of your mind, you're scared. Because you have to be.

Fear triggers the production of adrenaline, the hormone and neurotransmitter that activates our 'flight or fight' response. Adrenaline increases blood flow to the muscles. It increases our speed and strength. It sharpens our mental focus. It provides a burst of energy. In hunter-gatherer times, we needed these responses to help us survive in a world full of threats. To some extent we still do, but just as high-performance sports people know that they can harness the adrenaline that surges through their veins as they wait for the whistle to blow or the starting gun to sound, so we can harness it when we want to bring our A-game to a business situation.

Those same responses that helped us to flee a sabre-toothed tiger kick in when we step out of our comfort chamber and activate our 'do it scared' muscle.

> Smart people who lack courage end up bitter. Because they end up seeing less smart people with courage do better than them. Don't be a smart person who lacks courage. Act.

Doubt the doubt itself

So far, I've been trying to persuade you that fear can be a positive response to a situation, and that doing it scared is a rational approach that can lead to growth and success. Sometimes, though, the fear can feel overwhelming. We need a strategy to deal with those moments when doing it scared is not possible because the fear has become a barrier.

For me, that strategy is to doubt the doubt itself. I find this to be a profound way of thinking, both in my personal life and in my business life.

I'd been single for a long time. I wanted to date, and I didn't think I would be a complete disaster on the dating scene. But still: I found myself feeling anxious when talking to members of the opposite sex, and it held me back. Recently, though, I've been following my own advice and doubting the doubt itself. This has meant analysing the doubt, identifying the reasons it makes you feel a certain way and challenging any preconceptions that may have led you to a certain conclusion. I realized that my anxiety with respect to the dating scene derived from a worry that if I were to approach a potential partner, I would be rejected by them. In turn, I worried that I would feel embarrassed or humiliated, and that other people would judge me poorly. I had no real reason to think that these were particularly likely outcomes, but we are the stories we tell ourselves. As soon as I asked myself *why* I thought this way, told myself that maybe I didn't *need* to and made a conscious decision to reset my expectations that actually everything would probably be fine on the dating scene, my mental barrier disappeared. I'm not saying that dating remains anxiety-free for me, but by questioning the validity of my more extreme fears, I allowed myself to reframe the situation, and – suffice to say – the dating situation has markedly improved!

> How to overcome doubts about what you achieve:
> Doubt the doubt itself. Once you start doing this, you'll have few doubts left. And you'll be free to achieve whatever you want.

'We suffer more often in imagination than in reality.'
Seneca

Challenge the existing evidence

I've told you about how, when asking for fees or investment, or entering the world of public speaking, I had to do it scared. I've also told you how, once I'd exercized that 'do it scared' muscle, it removed the sting of fear when I had to perform these actions at a higher level. I started out thinking I was a person who found it difficult to ask for money or speak in public. I ended up knowing I was a person who didn't.

We can't always talk ourselves into these beliefs. Yes, we can normalize success by working in Claridge's or defining the person we want to be. Yes, we can harness the power of positive thinking. Sometimes, though, our beliefs are stubborn. They are formed by our experiences and shaped by evidence. If that evidence leads us to believe that we are limited in some way, we need to provide ourselves with new evidence that will help us mould an alternative belief. There's only one way to do this: to step outside of that comfort chamber into a situation that directly confronts your negative assumptions and belief-driven limitations. This is an uncomfortable process, but a necessary one if you want to grow and advance. It means doing it scared.

> Life is rarely as scary as the worst-case scenarios that you rehearse in your mind. Get moving and you will naturally stop overthinking. Action is the antidote to anxiety.

Make the decision and trust the process

When I was running Fanbytes, we reached a stage when it became apparent that we would have to cut a bunch of our old customers. Some of them were taking up too much of our time and holding us back from focusing on customers with more potential. Some of them, frankly, were just a pain in the butt. They provided revenue, but the hassle factor was increasingly not worth it. As scary decisions go, however, this was a doozy. Terminating our contracts with these customers meant losing about 30 per cent of our turnover. That's not something a business owner does without a certain amount of apprehension.

Decision-making can be scary. We worry that the decision may be the wrong one. We worry that the end result will be sub-optimal. But decision-making is also a core component of business. When you run a business, you're faced with countless decisions daily. How do we find a framework for dealing with the fear of getting it wrong?

The key, I discovered, is to commit to the process and almost forget the decision. Once made, that decision is in the past. The end goal is at some arbitrary point in the future, and unknown. Your only rational behaviour is to acknowledge that you've committed to a certain course, and trust that process.

I have great admiration for people who decide, several months out, to run the marathon. They do precisely what I'm recommending here. They make a decision. Once the decision is made, it's made. They don't have to worry about it. They now just have to focus on the inputs, commit to the process of putting in the requisite training, and trust that this will lead to a favourable outcome: the completed marathon. We can learn a lot from that mindset.

I'm not a Christian, but my mother is, and I'll never forget something she often used to say. 'I will do my best and God will do the rest.' I always thought it was rather beautiful, and rather smart. At some level, my mum understood the need to control the controllable, and detach herself from those outcomes that were beyond her ability to influence. She was aware of the need to make the decision and trust the process.

> *'Worrying gets you nowhere. If you turn up worrying about how you're going to perform, you've already lost. Train hard, turn up, run your best, and the rest will take care of itself.'*
> Usain Bolt

I am just a moment in their day

If we overstate how much people care about the minutiae of our lives, it can make us fearful, and not in a good way. Recently at the gym, I saw a young woman loitering around a piece of equipment. She obviously wanted to use it, but didn't know how. With her phone in one hand, she was watching an instruction video on TikTok, but that evidently didn't give her the confidence she lacked. She started to step aside, so I asked if she wanted any help. The young woman was incredibly grateful as I gave her a few moments of my time. 'I just didn't want to look dumb in front of everybody else,' she said.

I tried to imagine what she thought people might think. *You'll never guess what happened at the gym today! There was this woman who tried to use the machine, and she didn't know how to, so she walked away. She must be a complete loser!* Obviously, nobody was going to think this. They had their mind on other matters. She was an insignificant moment in everybody's day.

In the previous chapter, I told you how my tendency to procrastinate led to an unfortunate moment when my laptop died while I was giving a big presentation in front of thousands of people. Awkward. Except, maybe not. Because, as I told myself that day, everybody in the audience would have forgotten about that moment within 24 hours, maybe less. How do I know that? Because I'm human, and I know that I spend most of my time caught up in my own thoughts and preoccupations, rather than focusing on the tiny blips of other people's lives. They are just a moment in my day. And if I think like this, it follows that other people think like this too. I am just a moment in their day.

We become fearful when we worry about how others might judge us if we fail. The truth is, not only will they not judge us, they probably won't even think about us.

You are just a moment in their lives

Sometimes in business you have to do something unpalatable, like fire an employee. Let me tell you about the first time I had to do that.

This person was obviously not the right fit for the company. Their work wasn't up to scratch, they didn't massively get on with the other employees and I think it was clear to everyone – and even to the person themselves – that they had to go. It was a bad situation. I made it no better by delaying. I put off the inevitable for weeks and weeks because I was too scared to have the conversation. I was scared for two reasons. Firstly, this was new territory, way out of my comfort chamber. Secondly, I empathized with my employee. Thanks to this job, they had an income. For that income to be suddenly removed would be very stressful for them, not to mention the sting of humiliation they would undoubtedly feel at being let go. I couldn't bear to see them being sad, or to think of them alone at home knowing that they were surplus to requirements.

So, when the time came when I was unable to put it off any longer, and I asked if they could sit down with me for a chat, my anxiety manifested in a physical response. My toes literally curled in my shoes. My stomach turned. The prospect of firing this employee terrified me. In the end, I just had to do it scared.

Now, it would be trite of me to suggest that this difficult conversation was simply a moment in the employee's day, a nothing event that would be forgotten within 24 hours like a speaker's malfunctioning laptop. Over time, however, I learned an associated truth. Having let other people go, as all business owners must at some point, I would occasionally bump into my former employees, and guess what? Their careers hadn't come to an end. I hadn't dealt them a life blow from which they would never recover. They'd moved on and got a new job. It was a shame things hadn't worked out between us, but they understood and it was no big deal.

Empathy is an unequivocally positive attribute, of course, but sometimes we over-empathize, and this leads us to overestimate the impact our actions have on other people's lives. The first employee I fired soon found another job. Perhaps they thought I was the worst guy in the world for a few days, before simply getting on with their life. And now, I doubt they think back on their time at Fanbytes with particular rancour, if they think back on it at all. So while that difficult conversation was not just a moment in their day, it was just a moment in their lives. If I'd had this perspective the first time I had to fire someone, it would have been a much less terrifying experience.

Not nice, of course. Perhaps still a little scary. But not toe-curlingly so.

Because you're worth it (no, seriously . . .)

A final word about fear in business. I often mentor people who have a skill in a particular area but feel scared about turning that skill into a business. This frequently happens when people try to build service-based businesses, because they feel fraudulent asking to be paid for something they're used to offering for nothing. For example, a skilled graphic designer might be so accustomed to giving his friends graphic-design tips that it feels uncomfortable to start demanding money for it from strangers. This sense of fear happens more often than you might think, and it's extremely limiting.

If you recognize this tendency in yourself, let me suggest a little hack to deal with this fear. You need to reframe the situation in your mind. You are not a blagger, trying to squeeze undeserved money out of an unsuspecting target. You are a skilled person offering a service that directly benefits your customer. If your fee outweighed the benefit to the customer, they wouldn't pay it. Thought of in this way, the transaction becomes less about you asking for money and more about your customer receiving a much-needed service, facilitated by you. You're asking for money because you're worth it.

It will still be a little bit scary at first, of course, but reframing it this way can give you the bump you need to do it scared.

> Don't let fear get you caught in the hesitation loop.
> You think of an idea.
> You don't do it yourself.
> You see someone do it.
> You still don't do it yourself.

That person does it well.
You then get annoyed.
Eventually you say, 'They have something I don't.'
You tell yourself a BS story about why you couldn't do what you wanted.
The cycle begins again.
Don't be this person.
Act. Do it scared.

The Cheat Sheet

- In business and in life, the more you exercise your 'do it scared' muscle, the easier it becomes to do scary things.
- Be constantly aware of our tendency to self-sabotage when faced with scary propositions.
- Expect scary moments to occur, so they do not overwhelm you.
- Get out of your comfort chamber!
- Remember that adrenaline improves performance.

- Analyse your fears. Identify their assumptions. Doubt the doubt itself.
- When we challenge existing evidence, we create new beliefs about ourselves.
- Once a decision is made, forget about it and trust the process.
- People think about you less than you might imagine. You are just a moment in their day, and indeed their lives. Don't be limited by thinking otherwise.

Cheatcode 5: Originality Is Overrated

I have never had an original idea in my life.

Everything I've done in business has been stolen from someone. Take Fanbytes. Not only was it an unoriginal idea, I arrived at it having experimented with a number of other unoriginal ideas. As I've already mentioned, the idea my co-founders and I first worked on was Bandzie. This was based on an American company called Prizeo, which gave users the opportunity to win experiences with their favourite celebrities. I saw that Prizeo had raised money in funding rounds and that it was also generating a lot of cash. My idea was to adapt this model for the UK market. It didn't fly, but in the process we found ourselves working with certain YouTubers and understanding the influence that they held. I also came across companies such as Neoreach and Influential, which specialized in influencer marketing. They were young and had good success in the US. I decided to take that idea and adapt it for the more niche UK market, and to niche it even more we decided to focus on Gen Z.

Perhaps you think that this lack of originality is nothing to boast about. Perhaps you think I should be sheepish about such an admission. Surely we all crave originality. Surely we would all like people to think that we are creative and maverick, that we think outside the box and are rewarded for doing so. I don't take this view at all. In fact, I take the opposite view. I think we should steal ideas and skills. Like Jay-Z (via Mark Twain), I believe that while history doesn't repeat itself, it often rhymes.

In this chapter, I don't just hope to persuade you that originality is overrated. I don't even hope to persuade you that copying others is merely a hack to get you on to the fast track. I hope to persuade you that a lack of originality is an essential component to success, not only in business but also in general life. And I hope that the ideas in this chapter will help you think in terms of being a *solution thief*.

Creatively reimagine what already exists

Being unoriginal is not the same as being uncreative. Some of the biggest companies of the moment are based on unoriginal ideas that have been creatively reimagined.

Take Uber. Not only have people been using taxis for decades, they've been using their phones to call taxis for decades. Uber's supposed innovation was the use of an app to remove the friction of having to speak to a taxi operator. There's no doubt that they improved the experience, but there is nothing original about the core service.

Airbnb originated as a couch-surfing website. Couch-surfing has been a thing since before you or I were born. Airbnb made it pretty, frictionless and easier for people to connect, but again the core service existed already.

If we look at some of the most successful entrepreneurs of modern times, we see that their success has been based on their ability to creatively reimagine existing business. Some examples:

Oliver Bridge

By the age of 25, Oliver Bridge had already launched a number of companies, including an online business sourcing oversize shoes for people with big feet and a website allowing people to check the likely gender of a name from anywhere in the world. In both these instances, he'd spotted a problem that needed a solution, and provided one. Now he had another problem: sensitive skin. He found he was spending a load of money on shaving products that left his skin sore, and he was inspired by a successful business in America called the Dollar Shave Club. It inspired him to start Cornerstone, a mail-order shaving products business for men with sensitive skin. Not a new idea, but an idea that creatively reimagined an existing concept.

Alex Chesterman

In the mid-2000s, many property websites existed. Rightmove, FindaProperty and, in the US, Zillow. To have started yet another might have seemed eccentric, since the market was so crowded. Alex Chesterman didn't think so. In founding the property website Zoopla, he took an unoriginal idea and gave it his own spin by harnessing the availability of house price data and making this available to the consumer. He didn't try to reinvent the wheel – he just improved it a little. A decade later he sold the company that owned Zoopla and other websites for £2.2 billion.

Will Shu

Will Shu was an American analyst from Morgan Stanley who moved to London for work. He found, when working late at night, that he was unable to order food to be delivered. In America, on-demand food delivery services like GrubHub existed. Shu took that existing idea and applied it to the UK market, and especially to restaurants that were not set up for the online economy. The result was Deliveroo.

Ray Kroc of McDonald's, Howard Schultz of Starbucks, Jeff Bezos of Amazon . . . there is an almost endless list of entrepreneurs who have had a massive impact by reimagining existing business ideas.

The Samwer brothers

The Samwer brothers are three German siblings who have made a fortune in business out of the concept of being unoriginal. For them it's not just a hack, it's a whole business plan.

The Samwers identify successful American businesses, then clone them for the European market. Often, they end up selling their clones back to the original business. In 1999, having unsuccessfully petitioned eBay to allow them to run a version of its platform in Germany, they went ahead and built their own platform. They called it Alando and at first used it to sell off their own childhood toys to gain some traction. It worked. eBay realized that it had a significant competitor in Europe, and it bought Alando 100 days after the Samwers founded it for the sum of £35 million. The brothers then started a ringtone company called Jamba and sold it to the US competitor VeriSign for £176 million. Over the next few years, they invested in German versions of YouTube, Twitter and Facebook, then they went on to clone companies such as Airbnb, Pinterest and Groupon.

Some people look down on the Samwer brothers for the way they embrace the unoriginal. Not me. Many entrepreneurs, especially in Silicon Valley, fetishize originality. They're only interested in finding that golden idea that's going to change the world. It's why so many of them fail. Perhaps if they were to adopt the Samwer brothers' mindset, they'd increase their chances of founding a successful business. And it should be noted that the Samwers' approach is not necessarily the easy option. Plenty of other German auction sites existed when they started their eBay clone. The Samwers' success lay in the excellence of their execution. Being unoriginal is not a synonym for laziness. You still have to do good work to make a success of your idea.

> Success isn't about being the first to come up with an idea, it's about being the best at executing it.

'Original' ideas are often the children of existing ideas

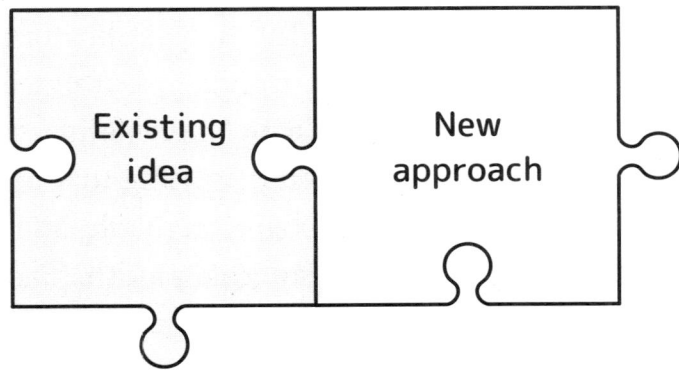

What we think of as original ideas are often the child of two or more existing ideas. Apple didn't invent the home computer or the operating system. Tesla didn't invent the electric car or the touch screen. I didn't invent influencer or brand marketing. I borrowed from existing ideas to make something of my own. We see this strategy all the time in the wider world, and especially in the creative arts. Any music artist you care to name will happily acknowledge the artists who shaped them. The same is true for novelists and painters. In these fields, the notion of generating new ideas from existing ones is accepted, even encouraged. There's no reason why this shouldn't be the case in the field of business. Humans have always generated new ideas by adapting old ones. It's how we progress.

I'd like to give you three ways of thinking about how to adapt existing ideas in order to 'give birth' to new ones. The first is to take an idea and apply it to a different geographical location – just as I did when I took the influencer marketing model from the US and adapted it for a UK market. The second is to take an idea and apply it to a different demographic. For example, onefinestay is luxury Airbnb for the very rich. The third idea is to look for so-called 'sawdust' businesses. These are businesses that use the byproducts or waste from existing businesses in order to provide a valuable product or service. A good example of this is a company called Oddbox, which takes misshapen fruit and vegetables that might otherwise have been discarded, and sells them at a discount.

> 'There is no such thing as a new idea. It is impossible. We simply take a lot of old ideas and put them into a sort of mental kaleidoscope. We give them a turn and they make new and curious combinations. We keep on turning and making new combinations indefinitely; but they are the same old pieces of coloured glass that have been in use through all the ages.'
> Mark Twain

Stop waiting for a eureka moment. Look around, see what works, and do it better. Improvement is more valuable than originality.

The two-step framework

What's the best way to find unoriginal solutions to the problems you might face in business? Is it through books? Is it through mentors? Well, there's no doubt that both of those sources of information have their value. The trouble is that most people go searching for advice from the biggest dogs in the field. If they want investment advice, for example, they might read Warren Buffet. No doubt he'll have plenty to say that's of interest. The issues with which Warren Buffet concerns himself, however, are likely to be far more complex than the issues faced by a rookie investor, so the advice he has to offer is likely only to be of limited value. I suggest a different framework, which is to consult someone who is only two steps ahead of you.

Let's say you have a business that is turning over £10,000 a month. Often, people will seek advice from a super-successful entrepreneur who has built a business worth £100 million. Chances are they'll receive lots of glamorous motivational blah, but very little in the way of actionable strategies to unlock the next stage in their journey. If, instead, they consult someone whose business is turning over £50,000 a month, they're much more likely to receive targeted tactical advice about how to level up.

I have fallen into this trap myself throughout my business journey. I'd ask advice of uber-successful entrepreneurs, and it wasn't that their answers to my questions weren't good, they just weren't relevant to somebody in my position. When Fanbytes started turning over £1 million a year, I signed up for some business coaching from a guy who had been very successful in the early 2000s. Everything he told me was valid, but almost none of it was useful because he was focusing on steps and strategy that were so far ahead of me. For example, he told me that I should focus on the importance of business culture. It might sound like heresy to say it, and there's no doubt that culture is important, but at that moment it was the least of my concerns. My biggest concern was getting and keeping customers. Culture could wait. He told me that I should be thinking about going global. To him it made sense because he'd just sold his business for £400 million and thinking globally was the norm. If Fanbytes had attempted to go global at that stage we'd have failed, because we didn't have a big enough team or a wide enough service offering. We'd have stretched ourselves too thin.

What I needed to hear was this. Until you have £2 million in revenue, your main focus needs to be finding a repeatable way to get customers. Once you've found a repeatable way to *get* customers, you need to find a repeatable way to *keep* customers. Without them, you don't have a business and at that stage in your evolution, you're in survival mode. Focusing on anything else is a distraction. The big dogs are likely to have forgotten this, but it's fresh in the memory of people two steps ahead.

Forget the blue-sky thinking. You're going to need to

go through the hard work that every early-stage business owner has to endure. The most efficient way to do this is to seek out and apply unoriginal solutions to problems that have always existed, from those who have recently experienced them. So, if your business has a team of ten, don't seek advice from the person who has a team of 100, seek it from the person who has a team of 20. If your business is doing £100,000 a month, don't seek advice from the person doing £1 million a month, seek it from the person doing £200,000 a month. (You can even apply this strategy outside of business, for example when you're looking for relationship advice. If you're 30 years old, you're likely to get much more relevant advice from a 40-year-old than from a 70-year-old.)

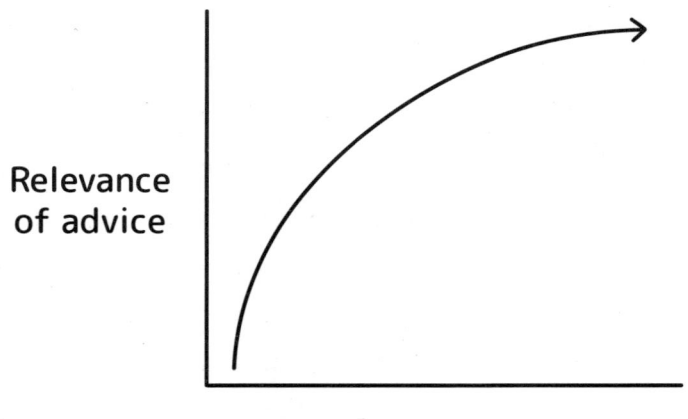

ORIGINALITY IS OVERRATED

Earn the right

We had an employee I'll call Sam. Sam was 24 years old, Fanbytes was only his second job, and his role was that of a campaign manager. Sam always wanted to come up with cool, innovative ways of doing things. He was forever proposing insane, creative ideas, and it did him no good. Like many young people, he over-glamorized strategy at the expense of process. His own strategy should have been this: to spend six months simply doing the task he was assigned to do, and doing it well. Had he done that, perhaps the rest of us would have taken his ideas more seriously. As it was, he didn't thrive because he spent more time trying to be original than productive.

You need to earn the right to be original. The Beatles had to record 'She Loves You' before they could make it to 'Revolution 9'. It's only when you have the time, capacity and money to experiment that you can invent the iPhone. Before that, you have to be a little bit shameless and maybe even a little bit boring.

I see a lot of young people trying to come up with fancy concepts in the course of their jobs. They fetishize the new and obsess about the notion that their brilliant idea deserves attention simply on the basis of its originality. They fail to understand that in order to learn the game, they have to start out by playing it the way it's typically played. It's only when you know the rules thoroughly that you can start bending them. Airbnb is a good example of a company that earned the right to innovate. If you search Airbnb now, you'll see all manner of quirky accommodation: log cabins, former film sets, castles. If they had started out offering these types of accommodation, they'd have flopped at the very beginning.

One of my favourite footballers is Luka Modric. I put him in a category with other greats like Paul Scholes, Patrick Vieira, even Frank Lampard. The reason they're great is not because they're flashy, but because they do the simple things well. They get the ball, they move it along, they bring people into play. You rarely see a display of ostentatious skill. From time to time, of course, they have their Hollywood moment and ping in a 40-yarder. But if Modric et al had only ever focused on the Hollywood moments, chances are they'd never have been professional footballers at all. If they hadn't learned to do the basic, boring, unoriginal stuff well, they'd never have earned the right to shoot for glory.

Originality is overrated because if people focus on it too heavily and too early, they lose sight of the fact that

ORIGINALITY IS OVERRATED

it's the successful execution of the more routine aspects of life that earn us the opportunity to do something different. Concentrate on the fundamentals, not the flashy. Concentrate on getting stuff done.

> *'Just learn how to get stuff done. I've seen at every level people who are very good at describing problems [. . .] describing why something went wrong or why something can't get fixed [. . .] A lot of times, the best way to get attention is: whatever is assigned to you, you are just nailing.'*
> Barack Obama

Let the algorithm do the work

Because of my background, I'm often asked by friends and acquaintances how they should build their audience on social media. My answer is always the same: don't try to be original. On TikTok, for example, look at videos similar to the content you want to make that have had a large number of hits, and copy that format. If you obsess about originality, chances are you'll have a tiny audience. If you emulate what's known to work, the algorithm will do the heavy lifting for you. Don't let your desire to come across like a creative social media genius cloud your judgement and blind you to your actual goal.

It can be easy to make this mistake. I've done it myself. When I started to work on my own personal brand and building my own audience, I focused on content and formats that made sense to me. Progress was slow. It was only when I took my own advice that my audience grew. The algorithm had shown that it favoured certain types of content. As soon as I started to make that content, things took off.

Confirmation bias

The cognitive psychologist Peter Wason pinpoints a bias to which we are particularly subject: the confirmation bias. It leads us, I think, to overrate the importance of originality.

Confirmation bias occurs when we interpret information in such a way that it confirms our prior beliefs, while we ignore information that challenges those beliefs. For example, if we have it in our heads that there are an unusually large number of orange cars on the road, our belief will be confirmed every time we see an orange car, but we'll tend to ignore the massive number of red cars. If we believe the received wisdom that originality is important, every time we see an original product, or are wowed by a piece of inspired thinking, we'll have that notion reinforced. We'll tend to ignore the huge quantity of unoriginal products or ideas on which modern life is built. The iPhone is an original idea. Every time we see one, it confirms the dubious notion that originality is always good. But we tend not to be wowed by the sight of plumbers' merchants, fast-food restaurants or scaffolding businesses – all completely unoriginal but quite possibly extremely lucrative businesses.

Copying is the shortest path to mastery

Early in his career, Leonardo da Vinci spent years studying and copying the works of all the great artists who had preceded him. The young Beethoven emulated the works of Haydn and Mozart. The Beatles sang cover songs. Bruce Lee perfected the techniques of various martial arts before developing his own style, Jeet Kune Do. Linus Torvalds perfected his understanding of existing operating systems before developing Linux.

All these innovators copied the work of those who went before them in order to achieve mastery in a particular field, and so create something of lasting value. I've noticed, though, that people often seem ashamed of the idea of copying another person. Too often, they conflate the idea of copying a person's work with the notion of wanting to be like that person. It's flawed, of course, because a person is not only defined by their work, but by their personality and situation, and a thousand other factors that make them who they are. A better way to think about copying a person's work is to adopt the mindset that Leonardo da Vinci, Beethoven, The Beatles, Bruce Lee and Linus Torvalds would surely have adopted: I am copying this person so I can be better at this skill. If you want to be a writer, copy good writers. If you want to be a good hairdresser, copy good hairdressers. If you want to be a good entrepreneur, copy good entrepreneurs. It's the shortest path to mastery.

One of the ways Fanbytes grew was through webinars and physical events where I would take to the stage and try to sell our concept. To start with, I sucked at it. I didn't know what I was doing. Then I came across 'Perfect Webinar' by Russell Brunson. It's a step-by-step method for creating the perfect webinar and selling on stage. One day we did an event for fashion brands, and I decided to follow the 'Perfect Webinar' model word for word. From that one talk, we sold £400,000 of bookings.

ORIGINALITY IS OVERRATED

I'd struggled with selling from the stage for so long, and it turned out that the answer I needed to become an expert had simply been hiding in a book somewhere. All I had to do was read the book and precisely copy its instructions. Game changer.

The intangibles

At the start of this chapter, I encouraged you to think in terms of being a 'solution thief'. I'd like to give you a concrete example of how doing this taught me a valuable business lesson.

There are certain challenges that most people encounter when they are trying to build a company. These challenges often occur when the company tries to scale up. For example, everything might be working well when you have 20 employees, but as soon as you double that to 40, it's commonly the case that life gets a bit tougher.

I encountered exactly this problem in the early days of Fanbytes. We had reached a certain size, we were making money and we wanted to take things to the next level by increasing our headcount and going after more contracts. We soon came up against two obstacles. The first was that I realized that now the operation was bigger, and I couldn't be everywhere at the same time, I'd ceased being able to be the key decision maker. This was problematic for me. I felt the need to hold on to the decision-making process, but I just couldn't. I quickly realized that I had to empower others in my team to make decisions. The second obstacle, however, was knottier. Now that our staff costs had doubled, the smaller deals that had been our bread and butter simply weren't enough. In order to justify our increased overheads, we had to go after more lucrative contracts.

So we did. We sought bigger clients who, rather than paying us for a £10,000 campaign, were willing to pay us for a £100,000 campaign. We figured – not unreasonably, we thought – that we'd offer the same service but at ten times the scale. So, instead of providing 20 influencers on a campaign, we'd provide 200 influencers. It seemed like the logical way to proceed.

It didn't work. We had an unacceptably high churn rate of clients. Sometimes we'd source the customers and we simply didn't land the gig. Sometimes we'd manage to do a big deal, but it would end up being a one-off because the customer didn't return. I was so frustrated. Everything had worked so well on a smaller scale. Why was it all going wrong on a bigger scale? I tried to come up with my own original ideas of how to solve this seemingly intractable problem. I figured it was my job, as CEO of the company, to devise an ingenious new solution. It didn't occur to me that others might have experienced the same issue and already found an answer. It didn't occur to me that originality was overrated.

One of our investors ran a successful data business and one day I found myself chatting to him over a cup of coffee. I explained to him my frustrating problem: that we were attracting big customers but we apparently weren't able to service them in the right way. Either they'd fail to engage us, or we'd lose their custom after one job. 'Exactly the same thing happened to us,' he said. And he went on to explain what we were doing wrong.

Imagine two chauffeur services. One charges £50 to take you to the airport. The other charges £250. They both do the same the job. They both make sure that you get to the airport at the same time. They both haul your luggage in and out of the car. So what's the difference? How can one service charge five times the other, especially in a world where there is no shortage of taxis? What is it that makes certain people prepared to pay the premium? Does the expensive service get you there five times faster? Of course not. The answer lies in the 'intangibles'. Perhaps there will be a slightly higher spec car – a BMW not a Prius. Perhaps your driver will be wearing a suit. Perhaps there'll be some chilled water in the back, or maybe even a glass of champagne. None of these intangibles alter the core service. Both will get you from A to B in the same amount of time. But the intangibles will make all the difference for a certain type of customer who expects to pay a little (or even a lot) for a higher level of service.

When you're working with big companies and brands, our investor explained to me, the intangibles are important. They give the sense of a white-glove service, which matters to customers who place a high value on themselves. The difficulty I was encountering was the same difficulty many service-based companies encounter. The solution was not new or original. I did not have to reinvent the wheel. I simply had to do what many CEOs had done before me, and consider the intangibles.

That one conversation changed our whole approach. When we onboarded our bigger, higher-paying customers, we explained that rather than give them a report at the end of the campaign, we would provide midweek reports throughout. It was a tiny tweak for us, but it gave the client an empowering sense that they were receiving a higher level of service. We invented a category of

ORIGINALITY IS OVERRATED

premium influencers, from whom the higher-spending clients would make their choices. We developed a brand safety tool, because we knew how important brand maintenance was to big companies. Our core service remained the same, but the intangibles – despite costing us very little – added real value for our customers. They felt that they were receiving a service worth paying a lot more for. I implemented our investor's suggestion, and all of a sudden we were able to win and hold on to the higher-paying clients.

I suppose it should have been obvious to me from the start that I didn't require a new solution. I needed to borrow an existing one. Now I see the same strategy being deployed everywhere. The hotel room that gives you 'free' access to the spa. The restaurant with a view that charges you twice as much for the same meal as the restaurant down a side street. The slightly more expensive babysitter who spends ten minutes doing the washing-up when the kids are in bed. The hairdresser who gives you a pre-cut consultation and a cappuccino. These are all examples of businesses who have worked out that you can charge more by adding a little extra element of customer service – and there's nothing original about that.

The world doesn't care

We often want to be original because of ego. It's understandable. There is certainly an ego boost when you come up with an amazing idea that nobody else has thought of, or arrive at the sought-after solution to a knotty problem that's eluding everyone else. Later in this book I will expand on the idea that ego is the enemy, but for now let's just say that if we properly examine our motivations and the reasons why we require a particular idea or solution, it shouldn't be too hard to see that it makes much better sense to shelve our ego and go searching for the answers where we're most likely to find them: in the heads of others.

There are no prizes for originality, nor penalties for a lack of it. At the end of the day, the world really doesn't care if you're original or not.

The Cheat Sheet

- 'Original' ideas are almost always the child of two or more existing ideas.

ORIGINALITY IS OVERRATED

- Seek advice from people two steps ahead of you.
- Certain behaviours reliably reap rewards. Let the algorithm of life do the work.
- Some of the world's biggest businesses are based on creatively imagining what already exists.
- If you want to perfect something, copy the masters.
- If you encounter a problem, chances are you're not the first. It means the solutions are already out there. You can steal them. You don't need to invent one from first principles.

Cheatcode 6: Build a Network When You're a Nobody

When I was still growing Fanbytes, I found myself invited to a dinner at the Peninsula hotel in Belgravia. I walked into the room and I saw massively wealthy entrepreneurs everywhere I looked. At one end of the table was the founder of Shazam. At the other end was the founder of LinkedIn. Over there were the MoneySuperMarket and Skyscanner guys. I shook one man's hand and thought: I'm sure I know you. It was only after a couple of minutes that I realized I'd just met Jimmy Wales, founder of Wikipedia.

And I thought to myself: how the hell does a kid with nothing from a council estate on the Old Kent Road end up in a room with some of the wealthiest, most influential people in the world of business?

The answer is: by using the principles in this chapter.

We all start life with nothing in the way of influence or connections. If we remain without connections, we remain without influence. Without influence, we have no hope of succeeding in the world of business. So we have to build a network and, almost by definition, we have to do it when we're a nobody. The process of becoming a 'somebody' *is* the process of building a network.

When we think about networking, we might think about networking events. We might think about someone giving out their business card and saying, 'Let's do business!' I believe that this is a superficial, overly transactional approach to networking. In this chapter I hope to persuade you that networking is not just a question of adding names to your contact book. Anybody can do that. Real networking is a question of deepening your relationship with people to your mutual benefit. Deep relationships take time. They require us to consider the human needs and expectations of the person on the other side of the equation, and to work out valuable ways of servicing those needs. The earlier you start, the more time you have to allow those relationships to evolve.

BUILD A NETWORK WHEN YOU'RE A NOBODY

It's better to be known well, than well known

Real-life networking is not dissimilar to social networking. People fall into the same traps online and IRL.

Lots of individuals successfully manage to build massive social-media followings, but the size of that following does not necessarily translate into the currency that is most valuable: influence. You can have all the fame in the world, but if nobody is moved by what you say, the impact of that fame will be negligible. So when we're building our network, our goal should not simply be contacts at any cost. The aim of effective networking is not for people to recognize your face, but for them to think: here is a person I believe to be credible, reliable and worth knowing.

You're much more likely to have a fruitful long-term business relationship (or indeed any kind of relationship) if it's based on trust, loyalty and profound understanding of each other's visions, skills and strengths. These traits of trust and loyalty spring from connections based on authenticity, rather than from widespread, superficial recognition. So before we discuss techniques that you might employ to build a network, let's take a moment to reflect that we should aim for depth rather than breadth. We're not looking to be everybody's best friend.

Never ask to pick my (or anyone's) brains

Typically, when people try to network, they want to network with those who have achieved something they themselves would like to achieve. They want to network with people who they perceive to be 'above' them in some kind of hierarchy. This is completely understandable. Objectively, if you're an early-stage entrepreneur and you're trying to get in touch with someone who has sold three companies for nine figures, from a financial perspective you are of course the inferior person. We can't ignore the truth that people are all on different stages of their journey or that, superficially at least, they have more to offer you than you have to offer them.

Consequently, when they want to connect with such a person, they approach the relationship with an inferior mindset. They adopt the 'can I pick your brains?' approach, which instantly cements the positions of the two parties in the hierarchy. It tacitly implies: 'You are so much better than me, and I'm hoping for your kindness.'

Maybe that approach will work from time to time.

Maybe you'll attract the sympathy of a mentor who doesn't have much on that day. But it's not a sustainable tactic, because it offers no mutual benefit. It relies on the milk of human kindness, which is sometimes in short supply.

A far more effective tactic is to take active steps *not* to present yourself as the inferior person in the relationship. To avoid the impression that you are the person with the least value. To do this, you need to consider the following question: how can I provide genuine value to the person whose help I'm requesting? Because if you can present your approach as one in which both parties have something to gain, the outcome you want becomes far more likely. I speak from experience. Random strangers often contact me asking the same question: can they buy me a cup of coffee so they can 'pick my brains'? I never want to be aloof or unhelpful, or to rain on anyone's parade, but the truth is that this is not a compelling proposition for me. It involves me taking precious time out from a busy working day and the only benefit, from my perspective, is a £4 cappuccino. Just as I'm unlikely to receive a favourable response if I email Warren Buffet asking to 'pick his brains' about investing, the random stranger is unlikely to receive a favourable response from me.

So the question now becomes: what can *I* do, with

little or no experience, to provide value to somebody who has more experience than me?

Be a person of value

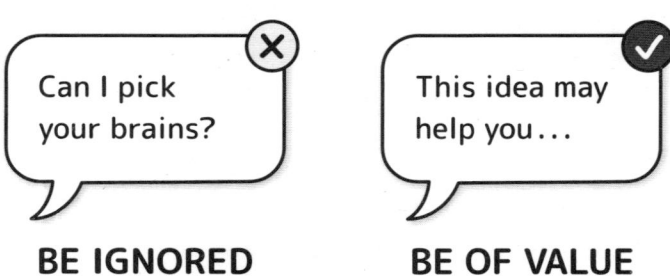

A connection is like an equation. It has to balance. And on either side of the equation there is a human. We need to acknowledge the existence of these two humans, and the very human impulse of self-interest that drives them.

You are acting out of self-interest in approaching a certain person, and that person is most likely to respond if doing so aligns with their own self-interest. Asking to 'pick their brains' won't cut it. A free cup of coffee holds no sway over a billionaire. We have to be more strategic in our approach. To do this, we need to deploy what I call the 'Money, Time, Expertise' framework.

In the world of business, there are three types of value

that you can provide to somebody, three levers that you can pull. You can help them make more money, you can help them save more time, or you can provide them with some kind of expertise. If you're able to say to a business-owner, 'Here's an idea that will make you more money,' or 'Here's a hack that will get you to your end point faster,' or 'Here are some resources that I think might be useful to you,' it's far more likely that your target will see you as a credible person.

In reality, the time and the expertise levers are going to be the easiest to pull. The most valuable asset you have when you are starting out is time. This puts you at a great advantage because in business, time is often the number one constraint. There are so many things that need to be done, so if you can save someone a bunch of time, you're already saving them money. But the way to do this is not to say, 'What is taking up your time? Let me help you!' That requires the person to think about how best to deploy your offer, which in turn takes up more of their time. The better approach is to study the person, come to an understanding of what might be useful to them and proactively do a bit of work that might be of value. When you approach them, you need to show them how you have *already* saved them some time.

As for the expertise lever, I'd like to give you two

examples of how I've personally pulled it to help build my network.

Russell Buckley is a well-known investor. When I wanted to introduce myself to him, I knew that he had absolutely no reason to 'meet me for a coffee' to 'pick his brains'. It would have been an act of supreme laziness on my part even to make that suggestion, not to mention an act of futility. Instead, I sent him some resources that I thought would be of use to him, based on my understanding of the world of social-media marketing and influencers. I deployed the 'expertise' section of the 'Money, Time, Expertise' framework. We connected as a result, and I like to think that there was mutual benefit in that connection.

I've already mentioned Alex Chesterman, the highly successful entrepreneur and founder of Zoopla. I wanted to get to know him when I was a 19-year-old nobody. How was I to do it? Send him a message and ask if I could buy him a coffee to pick his brains? It just wasn't going to happen. Instead, I sent him a message that detailed the big changes going on in the influencer marketing space, and how they could impact his portfolio of companies. That single message levelled the playing field. The difference in our ages became immaterial. So did the difference in our levels of wealth and influence. I presented myself as a thought leader in a very niche field and gave the impression that I knew more about that niche than anyone, and certainly him. I wasn't asking to be helped out, I was demonstrating how I could be of help.

A more high-leverage version of this strategy is to find someone who you think will be useful for your target to meet. You become the connector, the conduit. The bottom line, however, is that you need to present yourself as a person of value. If you come to a negotiation presenting as an inferior, you'll be treated as such. If you own something of value – you might understand something better than your target, or you might communicate in such a way that grabs their attention – and you present yourself such that it makes it clear you're not just looking for a handout, you will be treated accordingly. You won't be treated as someone begging for the other person's kindness, you'll be treated as a serious person because you take yourself seriously.

> The best way to get a mentor is to be worth mentoring. No one is going to hold your hand and walk with you out of mediocrity. Go do something. Look like you're trying and not just after a handout. That's where the magic happens.

Lean in to your core competency

A lot of young people assume that they don't have anything to offer (although if you've taken on board the cheatcode that Inexperience Is A Superpower, I hope you've been disabused of that notion). I've noticed also that a lot of minorities think that they have nothing they can bring to the table. Generally, this could not be further from the truth. When you're thinking of how you can present yourself as a person of value, you should look at things that come relatively easily to you, or things that you are already doing, then map out how those things can be of use to others.

As a business leader, when I was growing Fanbytes, I found it invaluable to have input from people who understood platform changes. As the company grew, it became increasingly important for us to understand more about YouTube, Instagram, Pinterest and the rest. Often people would approach me with information about recent changes in the various algorithms and what tweaks I needed to make to take advantage of them. These were the core competencies of people outside my immediate sphere, but they were extremely useful to me. I was able to use these insights to equip my team, and the people who provided them instantly became a highly valued part of my network. They'd proved their worth to me, even though they might not have traditionally been perceived as useful in a business sense.

Be a big fish in a small pond

The wider aim of leaning in to your core competency is to become a big fish in a small pond. You want to be known as the go-to girl or guy for a certain skill or knowledge set. The big fish in the small pond is much more likely to be noticed than the small fish in the big pond. I became known early on as the person who understood Gen Z. I didn't understand everything about marketing. I didn't even understand everything about social-media marketing. But whenever it came to networking, I was forever being introduced as Timo, the guy who knows about Gen Z. It made me realize how important it was to develop this core competency through practice, skill and self-promotion. You build a network by being known as a person who is good at a certain thing. That means investing in yourself.

> *'Investing in yourself is the best thing you can do. Anything that improves your own talents; nobody can tax it or take it away from you [. . .] But if you've got talent yourself, and you've maximized your talent, you've got a tremendous asset that can return tenfold.'*
> Warren Buffett

Do your research

A common question is: how do I make contact with a successful person in the first place? It's a good question, because most people make the error of not putting enough time into the initial approach. You can't just message someone with any old BS and hope that you land that longed-for coffee. It's a lazy way to think. This is likely to be a busy, important person – that's why you're trying to reach out to them – and the idea that your unconsidered approach will break through the noise of their busyness is for the birds. It's illogical – but that doesn't stop lots of people trying it, and inevitably failing.

Before making your approach, you need to study your target carefully. It's easy to do this nowadays. I have a strategy that I call the LinkedIn Likes Strategy.

This involves looking at what they 'like' on platforms such as LinkedIn. Often people don't post much on social media, but you can build a picture of their enthusiasms by looking at what other content they've engaged with. Even if they do post often, it's possible to build a more rounded picture of what might be likely to spark their interest by searching their likes. It improves your context. I have successfully used this technique myself to make approaches and improve my network. It has allowed me to identify topics that I think will usefully start a dialogue, and also to present myself in the right way to a person who knows nothing about me.

An examination of their social-media profiles will also help you gain visibility when you make your approach. There will likely be certain platforms with which they frequently engage and certain platforms with which they do not engage so often. Perhaps they're very active on Instagram and less active on YouTube. If you try to approach them on the popular platform, your message will get lost. If you approach them on the less popular platform, you'll have a much higher chance of visibility, especially if your approach is tailored according to your research.

The philosopher and businessman Ryan Holiday

has a technique called the Canvas Strategy. The theory behind the canvas strategy is that you should harness the power of metaphorically providing canvases for other people to paint on. You do the menial work of providing the raw materials, giving them the opportunity to be creative. Or, to put it another way, you identify the direction in which the person you are targeting is travelling, then you help them pack their bags to get there. Let's imagine you listen to a podcast where the person you wish to target mentions that they are interested in gut health. You might send them some articles and information about gut health that helps them widen their knowledge and understanding, without them having to do the tedious legwork of sourcing the material. Perhaps, on looking at their LinkedIn likes, you see that they've shown an interest in French cinema, or AI startups, or Cajun cookery. By sending them resources about these fledgling interests, you present yourself as a useful companion on the path they have chosen to follow.

Doing the research and then providing something of value at the first point of contact has almost infinite upsides and virtually no downsides. Your first contact is the fall of a domino. Hit that first domino just right and it starts the domino run. If you build a relationship with the right person, it can open up the doors to a bunch of other opportunities. And when you consider the exponential benefit to you of opening up new networks, you'll realize how stupid it is not to take the time to research your targets properly and get to know them in advance. A couple of minutes of research isn't going to cut it. This is an instance when it's important to over-focus.

The STIRS framework

Now that you've read this far, you're in a position to deploy what I call the STIRS framework.

Start a contact book. Create a Google sheet of people you want to get in touch with, a short bio and links to their social-media profiles.

Track and stalk them. Look at their social profiles and work out what engages them. This will give you the context you need to make yourself stand out.

Create an **I**nsight to a solution. Now you know what their interests are, you can work out an insight that's going to be of value to them.

Reach out on the platforms where they are least popular – there will be fewer people here, and you're more likely to stand out.

Scale what's working. Do this over a long enough time period and you'll build yourself a world-class network.

Publish online content

We've talked about how you might approach other people in the context of networking. That's only one side of the coin. You also want others to approach you. So, you need to ask yourself this question: how do I become a high-value number in someone else's contact book?

The answer is that if you are known as someone of value, opportunities will come to you. Nowadays, the best way of doing this is to put out content online. Most of the opportunities that have come my way since acquisition – and even before then – have come as a result of me putting my thoughts out there. This was the case even when I didn't have a lot of followers. Social algorithms are now sufficiently sophisticated that if you post about a specific niche or topic, and it resonates, people will find it. They will come to you because you're the person who has different ways of thinking and different ways of communicating. So, almost the highest leverage thing you can do to build a network – and this is true whether you're young or not, whether you're unknown or well established – is to start publishing your thoughts and ideas online. You never know who is going to be listening. And when you reach out to someone, and they are able to see your published content, it will give you an instant level of credibility over somebody who has published no content at all.

People wrongly assume that the aim of publishing content is to get famous. In this context, however, that is not the aim. The aim is to build authority and influence in a certain field. One of the main reasons people stop posting content is that they become disheartened at their inability to accumulate a million followers. Sure, a million followers would be great, but a thousand high-quality followers, among whose number you have actual influence, would be of huge value in the hunt for the person who might be your next client or offer you your next job.

Don't postpone yourself

I remember reading about a Google employee who left Google to start his own company. He was asked: what do you wish you had done more of when you were at Google? His response: he wished he'd made better use of his Google email address.

His point was this: there is a certain cachet that comes with being part of the Google brand and with being one of its employees. There is value in having yourself associated with that brand when you are building a network. This employee felt he should have leveraged the association more effectively while it was current, rather than waiting. I think it is very common for people to fail to do this. It's common for them to postpone themselves. They say to themselves: 'When I start my business, that's when I'll start to network. I'll harness everything that I've done previously when I most need it.' This is backwards thinking. You might be number 10,000 at Google, or Netflix, or PWC, on the very bottom rung, but there is value to using that Google/Netflix/PWC email address while you can, in order to take advantage of the cachet it brings.

Even if you can't harness a high-cachet association, this idea of not postponing yourself still holds. Too often, people kick down the road actions that they could easily carry out now, thinking that they'll only be ready at some later date. There's an old Chinese saying: 'The best time to plant an orchard is twenty years ago, the second-best time is now.' When you're building a network, there's no benefit to delaying. It's key to avoid postponing yourself.

How to ask better questions

My friend Dan Priestley, a well-known entrepreneur, taught me a tactic that has been of great value to me when building a network and a business. The idea is that when you reach out to someone, you should make it obvious to them that you are going to win in whatever endeavour you attempt *with or without their input.*

This approach immediately changes the dynamic from 'I need you in order for me to win' to 'I'm going on this journey, and it would be cool for you to join me, but it doesn't make too much difference to me either way.' The former dynamic immediately places you as the inferior party in the relationship. The latter is a much more powerful way to frame the approach. You're not ultimately seeking anything different, but the improved framing leads you to ask questions and seek advice in such a way that massively increases your chances of developing that contact.

Let's think about how this would work in a business setting. Imagine you're trying to build a meaningful contact with a person you've identified as a potential partner or investor. Here are two possible approaches:

- We're currently on £10,000 a month. We're struggling to get to £50,000 a month and it would be great to know your thoughts about how we might get there.
- We're currently on £10,000 a month. We're on track to do £50,000 a month. What was the one challenge you faced when you made that transition from £10,000 to £50,000?

The first approach is weak. It implies that you can't proceed without the input of the person you're approaching. The second approach implies that you're going to achieve success with or without them. You're on the road, you're going to get to your destination, it would be great to do so with your eyes open, but you'll get there anyway. Seek advice by all means, but frame your questions in a way that presents you in the most positive light.

There's deep psychology at work here. They say that everybody loves an underdog. There's some truth in that, but really everybody loves a victor. Winning is contagious. Millions of people support Real Madrid. It's not because they live in Madrid. It's because Real Madrid keep winning. People like to be associated with success.

They like the feeling of being a winner, and they can get that feeling by being associated with winners. So they're more likely to put themselves in a network with people they think are going to win anyway.

It's important to note that both approaches have the same objective: to build your network in a positive, impactful way. One approach, though, is much more likely to be successful than the other. The framing really matters.

Stop saying sorry

Tone matters too. I think people often imagine that there are killer sentences, key turns of phrase that form the perfect opening gambit and suddenly unlock a wide-reaching network. There are no such phrases. It's a question of mindset. However, tone is important. There are plenty of phrases that you *shouldn't* use. We should not sound apologetic for our approach. 'Sorry for taking up your time . . .' 'I know you must be busy . . .' 'I was hoping you might . . .' 'It would be good to connect at some point . . .' These kinds of phrases are non-committal and instantly present you as being the less important party.

The good news is that almost everybody falls into

the trap of phrasing their approaches in these ways. You don't have to make a big change in order to stand out. The bar is set very low.

Fake it till you make it (but be aware that you haven't made it)

If you frame your questions in such a way that you refuse to sound apologetic and present a 'with or without you' energy, there's an extent to which you're faking it till you make it. But you're probably wondering if there's a risk that you might come across in the wrong way. And that *is* a risk. Arrogance is an unattractive trait and will repel potential contacts rather than attracting them. So how do we guard against it?

The answer, I think, is not to pretend that you are higher up the business hierarchy than is actually the case. It's to be constantly aware of your actual position, but to own that position confidently. For me, this approach consolidates the importance of leaning in to your core competency.

If I was to try to network with a billionaire using the ideas in this chapter, I would think carefully about what I could offer him or her that would be of value. If I were to tell them that I had a way of making them another couple of million, I'd hit a dead end because to them a couple of million is just a rounding error. It would be absurd for me to pretend that I was trying to connect with them as a business equal. But if I can own my place in the hierarchy by displaying absolute confidence in my core competency, I present myself as a useful person in an area in which the person I'm targeting has no expertise. There is no point in being shy and furtive about this. There is no point in projecting a sense of not wanting to overstep the mark. You're not overstepping the mark if you're realistic about your place in the hierarchy and you are genuinely owning it.

Target the second in command

There is a concept in business called the Dream 100 Strategy. It's the brainchild of Chet Holmes, who developed it when selling advertising space for a newspaper owned by Charlie Munger, who was Warren Buffett's right-hand man at Berkshire Hathaway. The concept derives from the 80/20 rule I mentioned before, which is the observation that 80 per cent of your positive outcomes in business come from 20 per cent of your inputs. From this, Holmes deduced that targeted sales techniques would be much more productive than scattergun sales techniques. The idea behind the Dream 100 Strategy is to draw up a list of your 100 most potentially valuable clients, and focus hard on those clients to the exclusion of 'great' but not 'dream' clients.

Dream clients, though, can be hard to access. The networking opportunities might be scarce. So, as well as drawing up this list, I suggest an additional strategy. Draw up *another* list of the 100 people who have some kind of influence over the people in your Dream 100. You then network with *these* people as a means of getting to your real target.

It doesn't have to be 100, of course. That's a big list. The concept works just as well for the Dream 50 or even the Dream 10. Let's say you run an e-commerce business, and you want to get in touch with the 10 agency owners in the world who best understand Facebook ads in your particular category. One approach would be to attempt to contact the people in your list directly and bring them into your network. You won't be the only person doing that. They'll be busy and you'll be just another line in their inbox. A better strategy might be to contact their number two or number three. These people won't have nearly so many networking approaches because most people will be focusing on the head honcho. Your chances of getting in with them are vastly higher. Moreover, you'll be harnessing the credibility and trust those people have with your target. Finally, you'll be able to leverage the fact that if you have something positive to offer, it'll put the number two in a good light if they take your offering to their boss. It's a win-win situation.

This is, incidentally, a great strategy for networking with celebrities when you have no obvious means of contacting them. There's not much point directly approaching a celebrity. You'll be one of thousands. Very few people, however, consider networking with individuals lower down in the celebrity's team, even though doing so is an obvious path to their destination.

Focus on the personal as well as the transactional

I was doing a pitch to a potential investor. He's a pretty high-up guy in the world of advertising and marketing. As I sat in the meeting, it occurred to me that, whether he invested or not, I was genuinely intrigued to know something about his interests. Instead of over-focusing on my pitch, I asked him what book he was reading at the moment.

That one question changed the complete dynamic of the interaction. I don't know whether he'd made a decision at that moment whether or not to give us the money. All I know is that by showing an interest in him and his influences, I cemented the foundations of the relationship. By giving him the – quite genuine – impression that I would value this relationship whether he invested or not, I elevated the interaction from the merely transactional to the personal.

Too often in business we focus on the transactional nature of networking, but friendly personal relationships are just as important. It's worth remembering this when you're starting out, because while you may lack the assets to make meaningful transactional interactions, you will never lack the tools you need to make meaningful personal relationships.

Assume positive intent

One of my favourite heuristics is Hanlon's razor. It states that we should never attribute to malice that which can be explained by neglect. This way of thinking appeals to me because it reminds us that, in general, people are not out to get us. If you haven't received that email you've been expecting, Hanlon's razor tells us that it's probably because someone forgot to send it, rather than for some more sinister reason. This heuristic is a great life tool, because it encourages us not to default to the worst-case explanation of an unwanted event. It is particularly powerful in the context of networking because it allows us to *assume positive intent*.

The reason this assumption matters is because it changes the way we act towards others. If you assume that people have positive feelings towards you, and that when you walk into a room they will naturally gravitate in your direction, it leads you to act in a certain way that attracts others. (We are the stories we tell ourselves.)

Throughout my years in business, I've noticed that I seldom have cause to change my mind about an employee. If I consider an employee to be sub-par during their probation period, I tend not to change my mind about them further down the line. If I consider them to be an average employee during probation, I'll continue to think that. The same goes for employees I think are brilliant in their probation period. My opinion, on the whole, remains consistent. I don't think this consistency of opinion is unique to me. How things start, in social dynamics, tends to be how they continue. First impressions matter, because first impressions last.

When we assume positive intent, and act in such a way that we believe another person has friendly objectives, we reverse-engineer this bias. By starting with a happy, friendly, give-and-take attitude, we massively improve the chances that this will be the default setting for the relationship. This makes networking easier to start with, but it also improves the depth and quality of the relationship, and that's what we're after.

The assumption of positive intent is also crucial when it comes to managing the boss-employee relationship, as I found out when I had an employee with whom I had to have a few conversations about her performance. After those conversations, she contributed to a campaign that didn't go so well. My initial assumption was that she had messed it up intentionally because she thought she was on the way out, and perhaps even to spite me. I thought I would have to fire her, and even scheduled an appointment to do just that. Then a member of the team took me to one side and explained that this employee was having a difficult time at home. Hanlon's razor kicked in as I allowed myself to consider the possibility that she wasn't being malicious, there was just more going on in her life. I asked my senior campaign manager to look after her a bit more and ensure she had all the support she needed at work. Sure enough, the employee's performance massively improved.

For you to win, I do not have to lose

As anybody goes through the journey of building a business, they will soon find themselves in the position of having to manage employees. It is worth remembering that employees and bosses are an integral and important part of each other's network, and that the rules of building meaningful relationships apply.

Assuming positive intent is key to the boss–employee relationship. Everybody makes mistakes now and then, so it's inevitable that, from time to time, your employees will mess up. Remember this: they didn't intend to do it. They're not out to spite you. Employ Hanlon's razor: never attribute to malice that which can be explained by neglect. The chances are that your employee screwed up because they're feeling under the weather, or they had an argument with their partner, or they're distracted because their car failed its MOT. This assumption of positive intent is crucial when you're managing people, because it lets you get to the heart of any real issues that might exist, and stops you compromising an important link in your network on the basis of a flawed assumption of malice.

A common point of friction in the boss-employee relationship is the question of compensation. If an employee comes to you asking for a raise, it can often feel like an adversarial moment. As a boss, you'll be highly sensitive to the economics of your business, and it's easy to interpret a request for a raise as a win/lose situation: in order for the employee to win, you have to lose. I can almost guarantee, though, that the employee is not thinking about it from this perspective. They almost certainly do not have negative intent. They're thinking about their cost of living, or about the increased contribution they're making to the business. They're not trying to stuff you; they're just thinking about themselves. If you, as a boss, assume positive intent, it puts you in a far stronger position to approach the negotiation from a place of understanding rather than ignorance, which is beneficial to the future trajectory of the relationship. Similarly, if an employee decides to leave the business, it's easy – and common – for a boss to take this personally, as if the employee has some kind of malign intention. It's easy to imagine that they're leaving the company because of *you*. A moment's thought will tell you that this probably isn't the case. It's far more likely that another company has offered them more money, or a higher position, or a job that fits their lifestyle better. A good framework in business and in life is to put yourself in the other person's shoes. What would you do in their situation? Chances are, you'd make the same choices. Again, assuming positive intent allows you to make the right decision for the ongoing health of the relationship. It maintains a healthy link in your network.

Assuming positive intent allows you to reframe the flawed framework 'for you to win, I have to lose' into the framework 'is there a way in which we both win?' When employees came to me for a raise, I would take pains not to be adversarial, but to encourage the employee to join me in thinking of this as a mutually beneficial opportunity. I would ask them: how do we ensure that, in return for a raise, you will provide more value to the company? If an employee provides an extra ten pounds of value, and asks for two pounds out of that, it's a no-brainer, because overall the company has grown. By putting yourself in the other person's shoes and not assuming that they're trying to get one over on you, you have the opportunity to increase the pie for everyone.

A network is two-way traffic

It's easy to assume that the only valuable relationships, from your perspective, are those between you and a person of 'higher' status who has something that you want. For this relationship to exist, of course, it requires a person of 'higher' status to maintain a relationship with a person of 'lower' status. In part, you can mitigate this disparity by using the techniques described earlier in this chapter. But for a network to function, we have to acknowledge that these different levels of experience and influence exist, and be as open to interfacing with people on the lower rungs as we are eager to interface with those on the higher rungs. We should be prepared to provide value to those lower down the hierarchy or at an earlier stage in their journey. (And from a more mercenary point of view, it's worth remembering that our positions in the hierarchy are not static. Careers tend not to be linear, especially now when it's so easy for a person to learn a new skill and change their trajectory. The person lower down the rung to whom you provide value today may well be the person you're approaching for funding two years down the line. By investing in your relationship with this person now, you're actually investing in the future of your network.)

Value isn't just financial

We've used the word 'value' many times in this chapter. When we think of the value of networks in a business sense, it's easy to make the mistake that we're only talking about financial value. I think it's worth highlighting that people provide value in different ways. We know this is true from our personal relationships. We all have people in our lives who will never make us any money, but whose company we value highly because they're funny, or calm, or empathetic, or insightful. These qualities matter to us. The people who introduce them into our lives are important. They add value far beyond the financial.

The strength of our network depends on the depth of our connections. That depth cannot always be measured by the position of the decimal point.

The Cheat Sheet

- The goal of networking is not contacts at any cost. It's to build alliances with people who believe you to be credible, reliable and worth knowing.
- When approaching a perceived superior, take steps to avoid appearing like the inferior person in the relationship.
- Invest in yourself so you can be a person of value.
- Never approach a potential contact without doing your research first.
- Everyone loves a winner, so present yourself as that.
- The best relationships are not just transactional, and you will never lack the tools to make meaningful personal relationships.
- Assume positive intent.
- The idea that for one person to win, another person has to lose is a flawed framework. Seek mutually beneficial opportunities.

Cheatcode 7: Ego is the Enemy

I once lost £230,000 in 30 minutes.

We were pitching for a contract for a particular brand, and the shortlist was down to us and one other agency. I found myself in a meeting with the brand's marketing director, and she nonchalantly asked: 'What do you think about the other guys?'

I bad-mouthed them. I said they were no good at their job and spread a little gossip. I guess I thought it was a smart move to trash-talk the opposition. It definitely wasn't. The brand made its decision to go with the other agency. A month or so later I met the marketing director at an event. 'It's a shame we didn't get the contract,' I said. She told me that when she'd asked the other agency the same question, instead of bad-mouthing us, they'd been perfectly complimentary about our strengths and had nothing to say about our weaknesses. Their response came over as measured and confident. Mine came over as personal, emotional and – crucially – egotistical. It gave the wrong impression. It was not a good look, and my ego came back to bite me.

Ego Is The Enemy is the title of a book by Ryan Holiday that had a profound effect on me. I want to make it clear, though, that although I genuinely believe this statement to be true, I'm not a fan of humility. If you are somebody with any degree of ambition, you have to believe that you are in some way different to other people. Most people I know would fade into oblivion if they were more humble than they already are. I think we should aim high and take credit for our achievements.

So, this chapter is not about telling you to get back in your box. It's not about telling you to temper your self-confidence. It's not about telling you to dim your light. If you can objectively and with good reason talk about your achievements, and not put other people down in the process, then do it. We need a healthy dose of confidence and trumpet-blowing to succeed in business and in life.

This chapter is about something else. When I talk about ego, I mean an over-emphasis on your own importance that can have negative outcomes because it stops you thinking clearly and objectively. I mean a tendency to let a belief that you have something different to offer descend into a certain arrogance. It's unseemly, of course, but it can also be deeply counter-productive.

Ego, left unchecked, can stop you achieving what you want to achieve.

The Mark Zuckerberg complex

If you read books or blogs or listen to stories about the founding of Facebook, you'll of course find that everybody talks about Mark Zuckerberg. According to the mythology, Zuckerberg was the guy who made it all happen. Everything was down to him.

Except, of course, it wasn't.

As I'm sure Mark Zuckerberg himself would agree, the success of Facebook was down to a whole team of people. COO Sheryl Sandberg, head of growth Chamath Palihapitiya, early investor and first president Sean Parker – the list of truly incredible people who provided crucial input to the company is long. Zuckerberg might have taken the lead, but the influence of the team around him was immeasurable.

What I call the Mark Zuckerberg complex is a cognitive bias whereby we imagine that the success of a company must be down to the talents of a single person. It's a common trait among business founders, and it's a trap that I myself fell into during the early days of Fanbytes. When the company only had about ten people, we had one particularly brilliant employee. He was smart, driven and passionate about influencer marketing and about the company. One day, he came to me and said that he was leaving. His reasoning was that he wanted to try something different, but I knew deep down that wasn't the real reason. The real reason he wanted to leave was me. I suffered badly from the Mark Zuckerberg complex in those early days. I believed that the company would live or die solely as a function of my decisions and inputs. It meant that I felt I had to come up not only with all the answers, but also with all the questions. I liked it when people asked my opinion, so I sought opportunities to give it.

This mindset turns you into a micromanager, and I lost this fantastic employee because of my micromanaging. I'd assign him a campaign with the implicit assumption that I trusted him to find the right influencers, but was then forever making suggestions of my own. I'd ignore the fact that he knew a particular client well, and made unwelcome and unnecessary suggestions about how he should present to them. I forced my input into his work because I succumbed to the bias that the company's success depended on me doing just that. As a result, I lost a good employee.

We are most susceptible to the Mark Zuckerberg complex when we allow our ego to feed our own sense of self-importance. Through the filter of ego, it seems like an attractive philosophy. It is, of course, completely flawed. The best companies depend on a network of talented people (the clue's in the word 'company'), and your own importance is not diminished by acknowledging the importance of others. You do not have to be a guru.

Ego stops you doing the grunt work

Nobody particularly relishes doing the grunt work. I know I don't. I often find myself knowing that I *should* be doing some particular task but reluctant to do it. I concoct a little story for myself. 'This is beneath me. It's below my pay grade. I should get someone else to do it.' I don't think I'm alone in this, and it's a problematic mindset, for a number of reasons.

Anybody who has achieved anything of significance started off doing the grunt work. It's how they learn the business. Ask any successful sportsperson about the grim, relentless hours of unseen training. Anybody who has travelled the path of entrepreneurship will know that, in the early days, it's all grunt work. When money is scarce, and headcount is low, you've no option but to do all the menial stuff. There is, of course, value in this. It is important to understand how your business works at a fundamental level. This does not cease to be true as you move further up the hierarchy. If you don't fully understand the inputs, you can't fully understand the outputs. I'm not suggesting that the CEO of a billion-dollar company should be restocking the stationery cupboard, but I do think that if you let your ego tell you that you're too important occasionally to attend to the more menial matters involved in running a business, you risk compromising your understanding of that business.

You also disempower yourself, and this is true in day-to-day life as well as in business. If you only ever let your cleaner put your washing on, the next time you need some clean jeans and your cleaner's not there, you're in trouble! If you think only high-level tasks are worthy of your attention, you lose the facility to attend to low-level tasks if the need arises.

> *'No one in New Zealand likes a big head. In the All Blacks environment there's no room for it [. . .] There are these structures in place, like the fact that we always leave the changing room*

as clean as it was when we walked in. So, you'll often see the likes of Richie McCaw and the coach Steve Hansen sweeping the shed.'
Dan Carter, All Blacks legend

How do you identify?

I used to give myself a lot of labels: 'Businessman', 'Entrepreneur', 'Founder', 'Boss'. In retrospect, this was a bad move. When you give yourself a label, you narrow your mindset because you assume that you are just one thing and not any number of other things. When we label ourselves as 'entrepreneurs' or 'founders' it can feed our ego, because we start to believe that we should only be pursuing the kind of 'high-level' activities appropriate to entrepreneurs and founders. (We are the stories we tell ourselves.) This, in turn, encourages the Mark Zuckerberg complex and makes us less inclined to do the grunt work – which are problematic for the reasons above.

Ego inhibits learning and growth. Business people – indeed any ambitious people – should continually seek new knowledge, and be open to feedback and constructive criticism. When ego takes over, it makes it so much harder for these desirable qualities to manifest themselves. Now, the label I try to give myself is 'learner'. It helps me build a sense of self not around my accomplishments, but around my potential for psychological and professional growth. This stops ego creeping in.

Ego stops us acknowledging that something can fail

I was recently speaking to somebody about my life in business, and he said: 'It's impressive, given that you guys started so young, that you knew what would work.' I had to tell him that the truth was slightly different. It wasn't so much that we knew what would work, as that we didn't know what wouldn't work. We had a healthy cocktail of naivety and self-confidence that meant we just didn't acknowledge the possibility of our venture failing. You see a similar single-mindedness in the Kanye Wests and Elon Musks of the world. Their confidence in their abilities is so strong that they simply do not seem to acknowledge the possibility that their ventures might fail. So clearly, there is sometimes a benefit to this mindset.

Unchecked ego, however, can turn this mindset

into something wholly negative. It's one thing to be uncompromising in your belief that your endeavours will come good. It's quite another to assume that your endeavours will come good simply because they're *your* brainchild. It leads us to believe that there's a predestined result, when really there's a whole lot of ambiguity and uncertainty to figure out. The times when I've failed to activate that objectivity and properly consider the possibility of failure have been disastrous.

I had an idea for a concept I called the Byte House. It was based on a similar concept that had been successful in the US called the Hype House. The concept of the Hype House was that a group of Gen Z TikTok-ers would live together in a big mansion and create content. My idea was to do the same thing for a UK market, as a project within Fanbytes. I allowed my ego to lead me to the false conclusion that it couldn't fail. I couldn't have been more wrong. The Byte House was an unmitigated disaster. I thought it was a good idea because I was a person who had good ideas. That was backwards thinking. A much sharper approach would have been for me to attempt to identify the ways in which the idea could succeed, but also the ways in which it could fail. The ability to make that assessment is clearly of huge benefit, but we compromise that ability if we let our ego get in the way.

On another occasion, I invested £50,000 into a company that I was convinced was going to work. It was a content marketing agency for financial data. I understood it. This was absolutely my sector, and having just sold my own company I was flush with the notion that my instincts were excellent. The investment was a car crash. It turned out that nobody wanted the product it offered, and no matter how much I tried to will it into existence, it failed and I lost all my money. I'd made the mistake of thinking that because I understood the business and it appealed to me, it must be a flier. My good instincts had served me well in the past, so they would serve me well in the future. My ego, however, freshly burnished by my recent success, had stopped me from seeing the flaws.

> The reason it's difficult for us as human beings to say, 'This is not the best idea,' is because we often assume that having a bad idea is somehow a reflection on us. We think: this is a bad idea, therefore I'm someone who comes out with bad

ideas, therefore I'm a bad entrepreneur. A knock-on effect of this tendency is that we might shy away from presenting certain ideas because we think that if they turn out not to be good, it'll be seen as a reflection on us. The secret is not to take it so personally. We need to acknowledge that, just because our idea might be no good, it doesn't mean that *we* are no good.

> 'We must be careful not to believe things simply because we want them to be true. No one can fool you as easily as you can fool yourself!'
> Richard Feynman

There is always another option

A friend of mine had a good job earning a salary of £130,000. She wanted to leave the consultancy where she was working and had an offer for a preferable job but at a much-reduced salary of £85,000. She asked my advice: should she stay or should she go? It seemed to me that her ego was clouding her decision-making process because it only allowed for two different scenarios: that she stayed in her current job and was successful, or that she moved to a new job and was successful. In reality, of course, there were more options: she could stay in her job and be unsuccessful, or she could move jobs and be unsuccessful. Given that she'd been successful in her current job and was likely to remain so, but that her success in the other job was uncertain, this reframing of her options changed the calculus of her decision.

Suppressing your ego and considering the outcome of your decision failing is not just an exercise in humility. It clarifies your thought processes. And a consideration of the worst-case scenario doesn't necessarily put you off the decision. It might illuminate the best route.

Ego can keep you in a rut

Ego can often be the trait that keeps you doing the thing that you don't want to do. I've noticed that many of my friends stay in jobs that they really don't like because they want to get to the next rung on the ladder. This is especially true in careers such as banking where there are well-defined career structures, and each rung brings extra financial reward but also extra kudos. You might start off as an analyst, then an associate, then a manager, then a director, then a VP. I have many friends who are a step below director, and although they don't really enjoy being in banking, their ego encourages them almost to fetishize that next step. It's a bizarre way to live your life, working hard to pursue a career that you don't want or like.

Our identity becomes bound up in what we do. We often feel that it might bruise our ego if we were to step aside and do something else that we may have perceived in the past as being somehow less prestigious. It keeps us in a rut and stops us going after what we really want.

I vs we

Ego is Latin for 'I', and in my early days as a founder, I became aware that I was using the word 'I' far too much, especially when talking about company achievements that really were team efforts. I decided that I needed to put myself on a training programme. I bought myself a counter and clicked it every time the word 'I' left my mouth while I was in the office. On the first day, I counted 73 'I's.

The language we use closely mirrors our thoughts. My overuse of that word reflected my ego. As soon as

I became aware of this tendency, I made a conscious effort to limit my usage of the word. Each day, the number on my counter reduced as I swapped 'I's for 'we's. This subtle but intentional change of language massively correlated not only with a notable improvement in company culture, but also with an improvement in accountability. When the rest of the team were made to realize that they were actually part of the business and not just there to help out, they became more willing to stand up and take on more responsibility.

Ego in a leader undermines team performance. It negatively affects morale and productivity. Taking active steps to tame that ego has a corresponding positive effect on team performance.

The alter ego (part 2)

In the first chapter of this book, we talked about the power of the alter ego. I'm a big fan of this concept, whereby we consider the traits, beliefs and habits of a version of ourselves that we would like to be and then, maybe even just for one day, exhibit them and act like that person.

One of the reasons that ego is the enemy, however, is

that inherent in the creation of an alter ego is the admission: I'm not there yet. For many people – especially ambitious people – that can be a hard truth. It requires us to admit that we are still a work in progress.

The Cheat Sheet

- The success of organizations is seldom down to a single person.
- If you don't fully understand the inputs, you can't fully understand the outputs. So don't tell yourself that the grunt work is beneath you.
- Unchecked ego can stop us acknowledging the possibility of our own failure, and so narrow our perspective.
- Labels limit us, unless we label ourselves 'learners'.
- Ego can make us fetishize jobs we don't really want.
- Replacing 'I' with 'we' leads to improved morale and accountability.

Cheatcode 8: It's Not That Deep

A potential investor was scheduled to put £250,000 into our business. This was a significant sum at that time (or indeed at any time). We'd drawn up a term sheet and the promise of this money massively informed our strategy. I hoped that he would be an anchor investor, whose commitment to our company would attract further investment.

The money was due to be with us on a Thursday. On the preceding Monday, the investor sent me a BBC news report suggesting that some people had claimed TikTok was in reality a Chinese Government spyware app. Now, TikTok might, like many other social-media platforms, collect user data, but it is most definitely *not* a Chinese Government spyware app. It was, however, an important part of our influencer-marketing offering. We were making a lot of money from TikTok campaigns. I replied to the investor, saying that this was generic Western anti-Chinese hyperbole. Because that's what it was.

On Tuesday, however, the investor got in touch with a long lecture about how China had always been trying to depose the West. As a result, he couldn't invest because he thought he would be investing in China.

What do you say to a man who has decided that investing in a Western company working with Western brands using Western influencers talking to a Western audience was in any way supporting China? It was beyond frustrating, but more than that I worried that this was the thin end of the wedge: what if his position was indicative of a more general anti-Chinese sentiment? There was a real chance that it would spell the end of the business.

There's a version of me that would have panicked and restrategized according to that catastrophic interpretation. And perhaps I would have done if I hadn't learned the importance of a mantra that has helped me keep matters in their proper perspective and keep my head: *It's not that deep.*

'It's not that deep' is a London term. It means that nothing is ever quite as important as we like to make out. It's a principle I only fully internalized midway through the Fanbytes journey. Before that, whenever things went bad – as they inevitably did – I would see it as a major catastrophe. It didn't really matter how small or insignificant the problem, I'd interpret it not as a bump in the road but as a proper disaster. When I learned to tell myself that it's not that deep, and to reframe any negative outcome as relatively just part of the game, I found that I became much more effective as an entrepreneur. I gained a clarity of focus and an ability to put events in their proper perspective. This is not only an important skill in business, of course. It's an important skill in life, for reasons that I hope will become clear in this chapter.

Now, some people use this approach to gaslight others, or even themselves. I'm not suggesting for a moment that we attempt to trivialize events or problems that are genuinely of consequence. I'm not suggesting that if a person is rightly angry, upset or scared about a negative outcome that we belittle or ignore their experience. This cheatcode is not a manifesto for self-delusion. Rather, it's a way of correcting our natural tendency to catastrophise, and of minimizing the knock-on effects of that tendency. It's a way of normalizing the apparently insurmountable, which gives us a massive advantage.

Three 'catastrophes'

To start with, I'd like to share with you three more events that occurred as I was building my company. Each of these events at the time seemed like a terrible outcome, to the extent that I almost allowed myself to believe that they would herald the end of the business. I think most founders will encounter similar problems at some stage during their journey.

Numbers falling off a cliff

We were fundraising for the business and were just reaching a stage when we expected some big customers to land. They didn't. As a result, our numbers fell off a cliff. The absolute worst time for this to happen is when you're trying to raise investment. I thought it was the end: we wouldn't be able to raise the money and the business would fail. Total panic.

But it wasn't that deep. We worked extra hard and the revenue picked up again. Rather than being an indication that the business was in trouble, if anything we'd managed to display that it was robust enough to thrive in the long term.

IT'S NOT THAT DEEP

The loss of an A+ player

An employee, who headed up our marketing department, received an offer from a competitor. She was comfortably one of the best employees we'd ever had, a sharp woman who absolutely nailed her role. I'd tried my best to give her the opportunity to be a bigger part of the team, but in the end she decided to jump ship. I didn't blame our competitor for poaching her, and I didn't blame her for making that decision. But I did worry. One of our secret sauces at Fanbytes was the excellence of our marketing and our ability to acquire customers profitably. I thought that having a marketing person go to a competitor meant that we'd lose that edge. This could have caused us real problems.

But it's not that deep. We tend to overstate the importance of relatively minor shifts. We are wired to imagine a string of negative consequences – if *that* happens, then *this* will happen, then *this* will happen – when in fact that string of consequences is one of a vast number of potential outcomes, almost all of which by definition end up not happening. It turned out there were a host of other attributes that made Fanbytes unique that our competitor was unable to replicate. The loss of an A+ player was a blow, but not the catastrophe I first feared.

The Snapchat pivot

Early on in the Fanbytes journey, we used to spend a lot of money on Snapchat influencers. That was our bread and butter. Then Snapchat changed their algorithm, which meant that the reach and engagement we previously commanded plummeted almost overnight. When this first happened, I thought it was the end. I remember sitting in the room with my co-founders wondering how we could re-imagine the company now that our principal offering was no more. Maybe we needed to pivot into e-commerce, or find some other way of making money as a company. Maybe we needed to completely change what we were doing.

Thank goodness we were able to say: 'It's not that deep.' There will always be difficult moments like this during a business's trajectory. It's of course possible that some of them will be terminal, but actually most of them will not be. The reason for this is that there are very few elements in business that actually matter . . .

The three elements that matter in business

As entrepreneurs, we can become over-enamoured with the idea that every aspect of our business has to be perfect. We need to get our team structure just right. Our finances have to be in the best shape possible. We have to have a well-defined company culture, slick branding and a cool website. None of this is true. To be successful in business, all you *really* need is:

1. A product or service that people want
2. A way to get customers
3. A way to keep customers.

These are not trivial necessities. Finding a product or service that people want is the hardest thing to do because so often we go with our *sense* of what people want rather than following what the data is telling us. However, once we have these three components sorted, everything else is bells and whistles. To illustrate this, I'd like to tell you about some PPP masks and a superhero otter.

During Covid, I knew a lot of people who made a lot of money because they happened to be in a position to supply PPP masks to healthcare providers. I won't mince my words: these were often not very smart people. Their teams – if they even had a team – were chaotic. Their company finances were an absolute mess. Company culture? Forget it. But: everyone was desperate for masks, and they knew how to source and deliver them at a price people were prepared to pay. They could certainly have optimized their operation, but the fundamentals of a profitable business were there.

In the early days of Fanbytes, I decided that we needed a mascot for our branding. I'd noticed that Reddit used an alien, and other companies had similarly quirky branding. At the time, I happened to be dating a woman whose favourite animal was an otter. I decided that this would be our mascot. But hang on! An otter by itself didn't seem quirky enough, so I turned it into a superhero otter. I thought that this kooky little image would encourage people to buy into our brand. My reasoning was dumb, and so was the mascot. A superhero otter made absolutely no sense at all. It was not good branding. But it's not that deep. In our first year, we turned over £400,000, with a superhero otter as our logo. We raised money from serious investors with a freakin' otter on our pitch deck! It didn't matter, because we'd made something that people wanted.

In business, we spend a lot of time sweating over things that turn out not to be all that important. The three components that matter, really matter. The rest of it? It's not that deep.

Will it matter in 48 hours?

I'm not suggesting that we ignore every problem we encounter. Saying 'It's not that deep' won't always be appropriate. We need a framework to decide what requires our attention and what we can safely dismiss. My strategy is to ask myself: will this matter in 48 hours?

Just as there are very few components over the long-term cycle of a business that actually matter, so there are very few moments that truly matter over the period of a day, a week or a month. We can't let ourselves get hung up on the tiny obstacles that we encounter during the day-to-day. Too often, people allow minor problems to infect the rest of their day. Asking yourself if a problem will matter in 48 hours allows you to triage any issues that present themselves. If it will matter in 48 hours, pay attention to it. If it won't matter . . . it's not that deep.

WHAT'S STOPPING YOU?

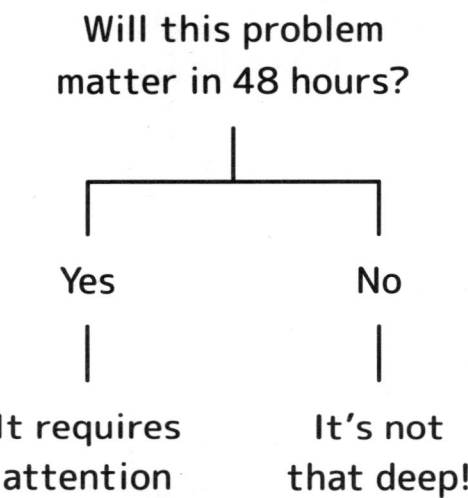

If you had £86,400, and someone stole £20 of it, would you then say: 'Since someone stole £20, my remaining £86,380 is worthless!'? I'm certain you wouldn't. Our time is much more precious than our money. In each day we have 86,400 seconds. If someone steals 20 of those seconds through an obnoxious comment or a thoughtless act, why would we allow it to ruin the remaining 86,380 seconds?

Your business is there to serve you

From a macro perspective, businesses themselves are much less important than your health, your family and your close friends. I think we all implicitly know this, but I've noticed that there is a strange and pervasive sense of martyrdom in the business world. Entrepreneurs often have a mindset of self-sacrifice. A mindset that says: 'I need to give up everything for my business, because that's what we do as entrepreneurs. I need to put it on a pedestal, above all else.' Frankly, it's a stupid way to approach the world. Your business is there to serve you. You are not there to serve it.

You can, at any time and of course within reason, stop doing the thing that you're doing. If you're learning to paddle board and you're not enjoying it, you can stop learning. If you're eating a meal and it doesn't taste good, you can stop eating. The same goes for business. If you're running a business and it's really not doing it for you any more, you can simply stop. If this feels like an uncomfortable truth, it's because we have, in the Western world, a crazy view of quitting. It's seen as something negative, as if it's evidence of weakness. In fact, as anyone who has ever broken up with a partner or found themselves in a position where they have to withdraw from a toxic relationship with a friend, quitting takes a great deal of courage. We need to reframe quitting not as a negative cop-out, but as an active decision to improve our life.

One of our cheatcodes is Ego is the Enemy and, as we've discussed in that chapter, ego sometimes causes people to stick with jobs they don't love. Ego, I think, also causes entrepreneurs to adopt a mindset of 'my business is my baby'. Whenever I hear someone describe their business in these terms, alarm bells ring. It means that the entrepreneur is thinking emotionally, not logically. That way of thinking clouds your judgement. It compromises clarity of thought because when we think emotionally, we overestimate the importance of minor problems. It makes it harder to say to ourselves, 'It's not that deep' and stops us separating the important issues from the trivial ones.

> Consider the Goldilocks principle to desire: you need to want it, but not too much. If you lack desire, you won't be particularly motivated to succeed, and the chances are you won't. But if you want it *too* much, and the thought of not

succeeding is horrific, you'll put obstacles in your way: stress, fear and anxiety. These obstacles can severely inhibit your performance. We perform best when we have nothing to lose, not when we have everything to lose. Saying 'It's not that deep' is a useful tool when applying the Goldilocks principle, because we often think that the consequences of failure are far worse than they really are.

Hanlon's razor revisited

We've discussed Hanlon's razor in the context of assuming positive intent. It's the heuristic that states that we should never attribute to malice that which can be explained by neglect. We can often feel like people are out to sabotage our endeavours, which can lead us to draw false conclusions and enact flawed solutions. But really, it's not that deep.

We had an employee who didn't see eye to eye with the rest of the team. His behaviour came across as disdainful and uncommitted. When he failed to complete a task we'd assigned him, one of my team approached me at lunch to complain about him. 'He's an idiot,' they said. 'He's stupid. He thinks he's on his way out, so he's sabotaging us.' Everything they said made sense. It was a logical, plausible argument that fitted the facts, and I was more than half inclined to believe it. But then I thought: maybe it's not that deep. I presented a counterargument. What if the employee in question had no ill intent? What if he didn't realize he was being obnoxious? What if, being young, he didn't fully understand professional decorum? What if he suffered from lapses in concentration, or some kind of neurodiversity that made things harder for him? It struck me that all these were at least as likely as, and probably more likely than, the interpretation of sabotage and ill-intent. And if that was the case, who was in the wrong for giving him that particular task? Probably us. By applying Hanlon's razor and thinking 'It's not that deep', we often allow ourselves an improved perspective on a problem.

It's only a point

In 2024, the tennis player Roger Federer gave a commencement speech to the graduating class of Dartmouth College. In this speech, he explained that in the 1,526 singles matches he played in his career, he won almost 80 per cent of those matches. When it came to points, it was a different story: he won only 54 per cent. He taught himself to think: 'It's only a point.'

Does that mean that each point is unimportant? Not at all. 'When you're playing a point,' he says, 'it's the most important thing in the world. But when it's behind you, it's behind you. This mindset is really crucial, because it frees you to fully commit to the next point, and the next one after that, with intensity, clarity and focus.'

Roger Federer's approach can be directly translated to business and to life. When we give ourselves permission to say 'It's not that deep' we are not negating the importance of a particular action. We're not saying that we shouldn't fully commit to it. We're ensuring that we don't allow small obstacles to hinder our future progress and growth. Because, as Federer says, sometimes you'll lose. But 'negative energy is wasted energy. You want to become a master at overcoming hard moments. That to me is the sign of a champion.'

You're the driver, not the car

When things go wrong, it's easy to assume that it's because you've done something wrong. Often, however, it's just the normal course of events, the natural ups and downs of life. Part of the 'It's not that deep' framework is allowing ourselves to distinguish between events going wrong of their own accord, and events going wrong as a result of your ineptitude.

I like to use the metaphor of a driver and a car. When you're driving and the car breaks down, you typically do not think: the car broke down because I'm a terrible driver. If you have a flat tyre because you ran over something sharp, you're likely simply to think: I must now change the tyre. You separate yourself from what is broken and figure out a way to fix it. You don't think: this is broken, and because of that I am broken. It's just not that deep.

If you imagine yourself as the driver and everything else that happens externally as the different cars that you might drive, you'll be more effective in business and generally live a more peaceful life.

Premeditatio malorum

Much of the angst we experience in life comes from unexpected challenges. When troubles hit you out of the blue, it can be difficult to say, 'It's not that deep.' It may even be wrong. But we can soften the impact of these challenges by anticipating them. This is the stoic principle of *premeditatio malorum*: the premeditation of evils.

I don't want to sound morbid, but it is the case that at some point we'll have friends who will die. In the normal course of events, our parents will pass away before us. We probably will experience the break-up of a relationship. The stoic philosopher Seneca advises that we mentally prepare ourselves for these difficult moments, so that we can reduce their impact when they inevitably occur. We can do the same thing in business. There will be difficult clients. Investors will pull out. Employees will defect to competitors. You will have moments when finances are difficult. If we can anticipate these challenges, we prepare ourselves for them and remain composed when they occur. This puts us in a much better position to apply the 'It's not that deep' framework. It balances our perspective, allows us to take a pragmatic approach and helps us see that problems may not be as severe as they first seem.

There is another advantage to the premeditation of evils. Understanding that there will be bad times helps you cherish the good times. It also helps you endure the neutral times, and 80 per cent of business life is going to be just that: neutral. You won't be winning big deals all the time. Mostly you'll just be repeating tasks that you know to work. The stoic approach really helps you appreciate the neutral.

The tide of panic

A final point. There was a period, during Donald Trump's first presidency, when he said he was going to ban TikTok. We all know how that worked out, but at the time, almost everybody in the social-media marketing world was freaking out. Ban TikTok? Surely that would spell the end of our entire industry. By this time, though, I had flexed my 'It's not that deep' muscle so often, I was able to bat away this perceived problem. Whenever I was interviewed about it, I was able to say: 'This is never going to happen. It's just Trump on one of his diatribes.' And I was right.

When we teach ourselves to say, 'It's not that deep' we learn valuable separation from those around us who are losing their heads. Panic is contagious. If you can separate yourself from it by contemplating the possibility that the source of the panic is overstated, you gain the ability to think clearly and objectively. In the case of the panic surrounding Trump and TikTok, I genuinely wondered if I was missing something. I wasn't. I had simply practised saying 'It's not that deep' to seemingly big problems, and therefore I was able to check our human tendency to overreact.

The Cheat Sheet

- Saying 'It's not that deep' allows us to gain proper perspective on supposed 'catastrophes'.
- Only three things matter in business – having a product or service people want, having a way to get customers and having a way to keep customers. Everything else is bells and whistles.
- Your business is there to serve you; you're not there to serve it.
- Don't overthink other people's mistakes – they're probably not out to get you.
- You won't win 100 per cent of the time and, just like pro tennis players, you don't *need* to win 100 per cent of the time.
- You're the driver, not the car. A puncture won't lose you your licence.

- Normalizing the idea that bad things will happen – in business and in life – helps you deal more easily with adverse events.
- Don't panic – it's probably not that deep!

Cheatcode 9:
Your Internal Scorecard

'Would you rather be the world's greatest lover, but have everyone think you're the world's worst lover? Or would you rather be the world's worst lover, but have everyone think you're the world's greatest lover?'

That's a question posed by Warren Buffett, and I think it's an interesting one. It goes straight to the heart of how we think about ourselves, and how we approach the validation and good approval of others. How concerned should we be about other people's opinions if they don't align with our own happiness and success, however we define those?

The idea of an internal scorecard describes a set of metrics by which an individual evaluates their own performance, decisions and actions. It is the opposite of an external scorecard, by which a person's assessment of these attributes relies on the opinions and values of others. Most people – not just Warren Buffett – would say that it's more important to pay attention to your internal scorecard than your external scorecard. We should be motivated by personal fulfilment, integrity and honesty. We should be resilient to external pressures.

Hands up everyone who thinks we can live up to that ideal.

I'm afraid I don't have my hand in the air.

The truth is that the idea of living life solely according to your own internal scorecard is a great idea in theory but almost impossible to achieve in practice.

One of the toughest parts about being in business is dealing with the sense that you're constantly two steps behind everyone else. This is especially the case if you're a young person and in the early stages of your business journey. It's exacerbated, as we'll discuss later in the chapter, by the ubiquity of social media. I constantly felt bad for comparing myself to others as an early-stage entrepreneur. The standard advice – 'Don't compare yourself to others, because everyone's running their own race' – felt unactionable. When I hear people offer the advice that we shouldn't compare ourselves to others, I can't help taking the view that this is as close to useless as a piece of advice can possibly be. As humans, we are comparison machines. No matter how hard we try, we cannot help but compare ourselves to others. We're hardwired to do it. It's baked in.

I knew I *was* going to compare myself to the competition, so I had to find a way of reframing that comparison. In this chapter, I'm going to offer some different ways to think about comparison. It's going to be a slightly weird chapter because some of what I have to say will contradict itself. I take my lead from a book called *How To Live* by Derek Sivers, in which he presents a series of philosophies for living your life, each one contradicting its predecessor. I find this a powerful way to think. Life is not a neat, one-size-fits-all proposition. Sometimes it requires us to challenge our existing assumptions and beliefs.

The internal vs the external

It's one thing to acknowledge that we are unlikely to avoid comparing ourselves to others. It's quite another to fall into the trap of believing we are comparing like with like. We're not. We're comparing our 'internal' with everybody else's 'external'. Our internal includes our inner monologues, our worries, our self-doubt and our 360-degree view of our life's canvas. It includes everything there is to know about ourselves, which can only be known *by* ourselves. Everybody else's external? That's largely a function of what it is they chose to present to the world: it's limited in scope and carefully curated.

This tension between the internal and the external of course lies at the heart of social media. If you've found yourself scrolling through Instagram and enviously lingering on posts of your friends living their best lives, you're not alone. Those posts, though, need to be understood for what they are: highly curated moments in time that fail to represent the reality of people's day-to-day in all its complexity and messiness. Life is not always a beach.

Social media did not invent this phenomenon, however. Humans habitually present the versions of themselves that they want others to see, and it's impossible for us to know with any certainty what others keep hidden about themselves. Businesses do the same thing. They sell shiny goods and services by tapping in to our tendency to compare ourselves to others. They also present a version of their own success that does not necessarily reflect the underlying strength of that business. Just because a competitor *looks* like they're doing brilliantly, it's not necessarily the case. Like your friend who's always posting pictures of their perfect Friday-night cocktail, their external and their internal may not be fully aligned. They show you the shiny bits and not the shitty bits. We shouldn't succumb to the cognitive bias of thinking otherwise.

What working with Nike taught me about checking my assumptions

We had landed the fashion brand Nike as a client, and they were spending a substantial sum with us.

And then they took their business to a competitor.

I envisaged all kinds of nightmare scenarios about what would happen next. Our competitor would obviously be much better than us. They would turn Nike into a much higher paying client. Word would get out that our competitor had outcompeted us and Fanbytes would be sent into a death spiral.

Er, no . . .

I realized that I was making a bunch of assumptions about various possible outcomes based on my tendency to compare other people's external to my internal. There were many other possible scenarios. Perhaps our competitor would simply tread water with Nike. Perhaps they even undercut us.

Sometimes we can't help comparing ourselves to others. We need to be aware that we're doing it, and we need to be certain that our comparisons are legitimate and not skewed by false assumptions.

The theory of the obvious

Have you ever listened to a piece of music, or watched a film, or read a book and thought to yourself: how the *heck* was the composer/director/author able to create that? There's absolutely no way I could ever do anything similar. It's completely out of my scope.

I think that all the time. When I was younger, I found this to be a dispiriting line of thought. By comparing myself to artists who had skill sets I will never have, I framed the comparison merely in terms of their genius and my relative inadequacy. Obviously that's not great for your self-esteem, but it's also not a sensible way to frame the comparison.

I discovered this as I grew older and became more established in the world of business. People would often approach me with some kind of marketing challenge,

YOUR INTERNAL SCORECARD

with a problem that eluded them entirely. I'd often find that the solution was completely obvious to me. I'd be able to give them a workable strategy almost immediately. Similarly, I knew people who were very fearful of public speaking, whereas I (having overcome the innate disadvantage of my stutter) found that I had the ability to speak with confidence in public (even on topics that I didn't know much about!).

It became apparent to me that I had a certain set of skills that came naturally. I have no doubt that the composers/directors/authors whose abilities I found so incomprehensible also have certain sets of skills that come naturally to them, which help them create what they create. I call this the 'theory of the obvious'. What's obvious to you may not be obvious to me, and vice versa. We often have our visors on, which make us think: if *I* know this, everybody else must know it too. This can lead us to believe the associated fallacy: if somebody else knows how to do something, I should too.

How do we harness the theory of the obvious when we consider our internal scorecard? It's obvious! We should only measure ourselves in those areas where our skills lie, and not in those areas where they don't. If I compare my filmmaking abilities to Martin Scorsese's,

I'll always come up short, and the comparison is of no practical use to me in any case. If I compare myself, on the other hand, to people in the fields of entrepreneurship or internet marketing, I'll at least learn something useful. The comparison can be a foundation, a way of calibrating my abilities, and giving a sense of where I am and what I need to do to improve.

> 'Everybody is a genius. But if you judge a fish by its ability to climb a tree, it will live its whole life believing that it is stupid.'
> attr. Albert Einstein

Write down five attributes, abilities or insights that seem obvious to you but might not be obvious to everybody else. Perhaps you have a higher aptitude for cookery, or running, or writing prompts for AI engines. Whatever your aptitudes, try to use these as benchmarks on your internal scorecard when you inevitably find yourself making comparisons with others.

The Gap vs the Gain

I was watching a race during the Paris Olympics. It was a close-run thing. When the gold, silver and bronze medallists took to the podium, it struck me that the unhappiest person there was probably not the bronze medallist, but the silver medallist. He was most likely thinking to himself: if only I'd run a fraction of a second faster, I could have taken the gold. The bronze medallist, on the other hand, was most likely thinking: thank goodness I didn't run a fraction of a second slower because then I wouldn't even have medalled. It reminded me of something that I've learned during my years in business, which is that a lot of our happiness and sense of achievement derives from the point from which we measure ourselves. Our internal scorecard is subject to baseline bias, and our happiness is often a function of whether we measure our progress or how far there is left to go.

The entrepreneur and author Dan Sullivan encapsulates this idea in his theory of 'the Gap and the Gain'. In this framework, 'the Gap' is the distance between where you are now and where you would ultimately like to be. 'The Gain' is the progress you've made relative to your starting point. It's a measure of how far you have come.

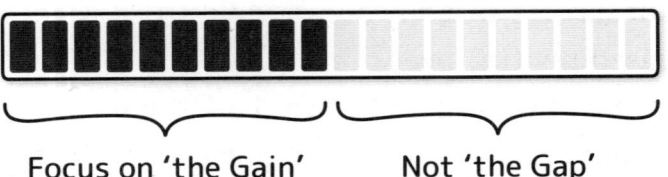

Too often, we focus on the Gap, which by definition means focusing on what we haven't yet achieved. It can be frustrating and demotivating because we're always thinking about what's missing in our life. We obsess about what is still out of reach and often fail to recognize our progress.

It's far better, in my opinion, to focus on the Gain. There is satisfaction and motivation to be found in concentrating on our progress. It allows us to celebrate our success and build our confidence. And it makes a lot more sense. The Gain is a measurable quantity: the metaphorical distance between where you were – a fixed point – and where you are. The Gap depends on imagining some arbitrary point in the future, some version of yourself and the world that doesn't yet exist, and may never.

I was guilty when building Fanbytes of living too much in the Gap. I'd meet other entrepreneurs who seemed to have it all (I know, I know – I was comparing their external with my internal) and beat myself up for not having sold my company for £100 million, or increased my turnover tenfold, or landed a big client. My mindset was all about what I hadn't done, rather than what I had. I won't lie: that way of thinking often got me down. I felt like I hadn't done enough, and never would.

But then, one day, I gave myself a good talking to. I thought about where I'd come from: the council estate on the Old Kent Road, the gang fights in Avondale Square, the gangster who saved my life. I allowed myself to think about how far I'd come and everything I'd achieved so far. I allowed myself to live in the Gain, and it made all the difference. Suddenly I had a real sense of growth and progress. By calibrating myself against my starting point rather than against some imaginary end point, I realigned my perspective and became more resilient to the uncertainties of the future.

Levelling up

Some people might think that focusing on the Gain rather than the Gap might indicate a lack of ambition. They might imagine that in patting yourself on the back about the past, you're not striving sufficiently for the future, or pushing yourself enough. That you're saying: it's not about how good I can be, it's about how good I have been so far. It's not about looking up, it's about looking down.

I disagree. Focusing on the Gain gives you the opportunity to express gratitude for where you are and to be aware of the next level up without feeling like a failure for not having reached it. This in turn empowers you to take the next incremental step without tying your sense of self to the necessity of taking it. This is important, because there's always another level, no matter who you are.

If we approach life as a constant process of levelling up, rather than a mad rush for the finish line, we set ourselves up for a constant evolution of success, rather than an infinite loop of self-doubt.

The inputs and the outputs

If we're going to compare ourselves to others – and we probably are – we need to ensure that we're comparing the right variables. In part, this means harnessing the theory of the obvious and not comparing our weaknesses with other people's strengths. It also means comparing the inputs, and not the outputs. This was a very profound realization for me.

Here are some examples of things we might say when we compare the outputs.

That person is richer than me.
That person is faster than me.
That person speaks Japanese better than I do.

All these observations may be true, but if you want to be richer, faster or speak better Japanese, they don't really get you very far. They're statements of fact, but they're not strategies. In isolation, they just lead us to think: oh man, I'm never going to get to that level. They force you to focus on the Gap.

Comparing the inputs is a strategy. It leads us to ask pertinent questions. What do these people know that I don't? What have they figured out that I haven't figured out? And consequently, what have they done that I haven't done? Most people aren't born geniuses. They aren't born wealthy, speedy or fluent. They've worked out a way to do it. They've managed to achieve a certain level of output because of a certain level of input. If you compare your inputs to their inputs, you'll learn something about what you need to do to match their outputs.

So, instead, you might observe:

> *That person has diversified their investments more than I have.*
> *That person has optimized their training regime with the help of a world-class athlete.*
> *That person goes to Japanese class three times a week.*

Once you've established the inputs, all you have to do is go ahead and emulate them. It will give you a good chance of emulating the outputs. (And remember what we said a few chapters back: originality is overrated. If someone has worked out the best way to achieve a certain outcome, there's nothing to stop us from copying their actions if we also want to achieve that outcome. We don't have to reinvent the wheel.)

Comparing the inputs rather than the outputs allows us to reframe entirely the whole process of comparison. It becomes a positive endeavour rather than a means of denting our confidence and putting ourselves down. It gets us on the fast track to where we want to be.

You are not Usain Bolt

Compare the inputs and not the outputs. Live the Gain and not the Gap. Check your assumptions. These are all smart calls for managing how we compare ourselves to others. But I said at the beginning of this chapter that there would be contradictions. There are some people who will achieve things you and I are never going to achieve. You are probably not Usain Bolt. I will never be LeBron James. If you compose music, you'll probably never be Mozart. If you write plays, you'll probably never be Shakespeare. Most people are not born geniuses, but some people are. Comparing your inputs with their inputs will only get you so far, because they're once-in-a-generation prodigies.

The health of our internal scorecard depends on our ability to approach comparison with others in a constructive way. Sometimes, though, we do just have to avoid the comparison. If we have no interest in being like a particular person, or no realistic expectation that we ever will be, the comparison is a meaningless metric. Don't get dragged into a race that isn't for you.

Woe is me! vs woah, it's me!

Comparison with others is often framed as a negative attribute, which makes sense if it leads to a 'woe is me!' mentality. You don't want the comparison to lead you down the path of thinking you can't do something, just because another person has done it so well. But let's flip that mentality on its head. Let's acknowledge that, in comparing ourselves with others, there's a little voice in our head telling us that, deep down, we still have something more to achieve. Let's acknowledge that the very act of comparison means we know we have another level we can tap into. Instead of letting the comparison lead us to say, 'Woe is me!' it should lead us to say, 'Woah, it's me!'

Beware the halo effect

As a teenager I became obsessed with a website called Retire at 21. It was full of information and profiles of people who had built hugely successful businesses and amassed vast fortunes at a very young age. I immersed myself in those stories in order to normalize the notion of success in my mind. I compared myself to those founders. I wanted to be like them. At some level, I felt a little bit worse about myself because I hadn't yet achieved their level of wealth and independence.

And then, one day, I met one of them.

And then I met another. And another.

And let me tell you, these were not the impressive people I imagined them to me. Some of them were drunks. Some of them were depressed. Many of them were quite unremarkable. I couldn't believe that these were the same people I once assumed were at the pinnacle of achievement. I couldn't believe that my mood used to be affected, for better or worse, by their stories.

When we work with our internal scorecard, and we compare ourselves to other successful people, we often end up placing them on a pedestal and assuming that they exhibit the same excellence in all parts of their life as they do in one. It's called the halo effect, and it leads us to ignore the fact that they are only human, and like all humans they have an immense number of flaws.

I find, slightly to my embarrassment, that young entrepreneurs do to me what I did to the Retire at 21 guys. They put me on a pedestal. They assume that because I've had some success in business, my life is perfect and everything is sorted. That's not the case. Like everyone's, my life has its complications. I'm neurodiverse, with OCD and ADHD. I have tics that are difficult to control. I have relationship difficulties and general anxieties, just like everybody else. Compare yourself to me if you like, but be aware that you're comparing yourself with someone who is very far from having it all worked out. Don't compare my external with your internal.

> Here's an African saying that I love: 'Do they have two heads?' This is one of the best phrases ever. It means that we shouldn't think other people are particularly special. Once you internalize that the people you look up to are no different to you, that they too have their own self-doubt and insecurities, your mind changes. It's like someone has gone into your brain, removed the curtain and said: 'Look! This is what you can do!' You realize that the life you want is actually very, very achievable.

The internal board of directors

In a business setting, the board of directors provides oversight and leadership. It ensures that an organization operates effectively and ethically. It ensures that the business operates in alignment with the interests of its stakeholders.

I have an internal board of directors. It only exists

in my head and comprises a dream panel of individuals I admire, and whose advice I would seek in real life, if I only had the opportunity. My internal board of directors do not all come from the world of business. They 'exist' to guide me in all aspects of my life. The board comprises the bodybuilder, actor and politician Arnold Schwarzenegger; the tennis player Serena Williams; the entrepreneur and business coach Sam Ovens; and the investor and philanthropist Charlie Munger.

Arnold Schwarzenegger

I admire Arnold because of his astonishing degree of determination and his ability repeatedly to remodel himself and build a new identity. To start life in a small Austrian village and grow up to dominate three fields of endeavour – bodybuilding, film acting and politics – displays an extraordinary level of commitment and persistence. To do this while maintaining a strong moral compass, devoting oneself to philanthropy and environmental advocacy, tells me that his own internal scorecard ticks all the right boxes.

Serena Williams

Serena is on my internal board of directors not only because of her dominance in the world of tennis. I admire her resilience in coming from a humble background in Compton, California to becoming a globally recognized figure. I admire her longevity and her ability to adapt to the changing nature of the game. I admire her physical and mental strength. I admire her entrepreneurial spirit and her positive influence on social issues, including racial equality and women's rights. She's driven, explosive, determined. I can't imagine a scenario in which her advice would not be of value.

Sam Ovens

Sam Ovens is the guy who got me into internet marketing at the very beginning. He has an extraordinary level of acumen partnered with a reassuring, calm demeanour. Most of all, I admire the way he thinks: his approach is always rational and logical. I know that if I were to consult Sam Ovens, he would help me think my way clearly through challenges.

Charlie Munger

Charlie was Warren Buffett's partner at Berkshire Hathaway, an incredibly successful investor and a true philanthropist. It's his perspective on life, though, that earns him a place on my internal board of directors. He has an ability to articulate truths about the world that seem obvious when you hear them, and offer simple, actionable strategies for living your life in a positive and productive way.

My internal board of directors are always on call when I need a framework with which to make my decisions. When I sold my company, and the sheen of being the Fanbytes guy started to wear off while the rest of my life stretched out ahead of me, it was empowering to think: what would Arnold do? I was able to think about how he reinvented himself throughout his life, and take some inspiration from that. But the consultations I have with my internal board of directors do not need to be about life-or-death, existential forks in the road. They are there to help out with much smaller issues. In the gym, when I'm struggling for motivation, I find that Serena has plenty to say. I was recently on holiday in Brazil with some friends. We decided to go out one night to a party place. I found myself surrounded by a lot of drunk, boisterous party people. I knew I had to be up early the next morning for some work calls, and I was conflicted: I knew I should head back to the hotel, but I didn't want to kill the vibe. I thought to myself: what would Sam Ovens do? How would he think about this situation? I decided he would observe that these drunk, boisterous party people were not conducive to the person I wanted to become. He would point out that even if I stayed and enjoyed myself, I would probably not get back till 2.30 a.m. and consequently not bring my A-game to my 8.30 a.m. call. And my friends would probably have just as good a time without me. With that logical approach, it became clear to me that there was no reason for me to stay, so I signed out early.

Your internal board of directors will not be the same as mine. To create your own personal board of directors, identify three to five people whose stories, personalities and actions resonate with you and whom you would truly like to consult in real life. Write them down, as I have, along with the reasons why they would earn their seat on the board. Now, model them specifically. Take one attribute that you admire from each of them, ideally ensuring that each attribute is distinct from the others, and introduce those attributes into your daily life. As you go about your day, you will have three to five specific benchmarks that help you make decisions. Being able to anchor these benchmarks to specific people makes them less nebulous, more concrete in your mind and easier to act upon.

Inverted comparisons

One of the main reasons Charlie Munger has a seat on my internal board of directors is that he introduced me to an idea that I call inverted comparisons. We've talked about the idea of comparing the inputs and not the outputs. This leads us to ask the question: if I wanted to be a person who achieves a particular desirable output, what are the things I would do? Charlie Munger suggests we turn this idea on its head, and ask: if I wanted to be a person who achieves a particular *undesirable* output, what are the things I would do? And then . . . don't do that thing!

For example, if I wanted to be unhealthy and out of shape, what would I do? I wouldn't exercise and I'd eat crappy food. If I wanted to go into debt, what would I do? I'd make sure I overspent my income. If I wanted an unsuccessful romantic relationship, what would I do? I'd be selfish and prioritize my own needs over my partner's.

It follows that if we don't want these outputs, we should avoid these inputs.

This gives us a different way of thinking about comparisons. We normally compare ourselves to successful people who have achieved desirable outcomes. We can learn just as much, though, by comparing ourselves to less successful people – real or imaginary – and avoiding their inputs. It's a powerful tool for our internal scorecard.

The Cheat Sheet

- The standard advice not to compare ourselves to others is impossible to follow. The secret lies in making useful comparisons.
- Other people's external does not equal your internal, or even theirs.
- Check your assumptions. False assumptions lead to skewed comparisons.
- What comes naturally to others may not come naturally to you, and vice versa. Only compare yourself to others in those areas where your skills lie.

YOUR INTERNAL SCORECARD

- It matters what you measure. Your progress is a far more useful metric than your distance from some arbitrary end point. Focus on the Gain, not the Gap.
- Compare the inputs, not the outputs.
- Populate your internal board of directors with people whose approach to life you most admire. Consult them often.

Cheatcode 10:
How To Get Lucky

Here's something you often hear successful entrepreneurs say when talking about their achievements: 'I got lucky!'

Man, it used to annoy me when I heard that. I felt completely certain that anybody who put their success down to luck was pulling the wool over my eyes. They were invoking this intangible concept as a way of hiding the truth. They *knew* what their secret sauce was, but they didn't want to share it with the likes of me. So they put it down to 'luck'. Who can argue with that?

Now, having played the entrepreneurial game myself, I realize that this wasn't BS. Luck has its part to play. When Napoleon famously said that he'd rather have lucky generals than good ones, no doubt he meant it. Some people, sometimes, experience unforeseen strokes of good fortune, and it's famously a flaw of the very successful that they attribute to their own brilliance what might be more realistically attributed to chance. But what I failed to understand back then is that, in general, luck isn't what many people assume it to be. Luck is not, at least not always, some random force completely distinct from our own structures and activities. It is not equally distributed. Luck is a function of those structures and activities. The amount of luck we experience correlates highly with the efforts we put in.

> 'The more I practise, the luckier I get.'
> attr. Gary Player

This cheatcode is all about how to engineer your own luck. It's about observing the world as it really is, and ensuring that we align ourselves accordingly. Our job, in business and in life, is to set our sails to catch the wind of good fortune when it blows.

My 'lucky' moments

I want to tell you about three lucky moments on my business journey, three inflexion points that put everything on an improved trajectory. In relating them,

I want you to take away the idea that they weren't lucky at all. They were just the natural consequences of certain behaviours.

During my gap year, although I had already decided that I wanted to be an entrepreneur, having successfully created and sold *Entrepreneur Express*, I decided that I needed to learn something about the world of business from other people. I reached out to the financial intelligence company Beauhurst for a sales job. The guy who ran the company interviewed me for the job and then said . . . no. He said he wanted somebody with a little more experience. Bad luck, huh?

Well, actually no.

Because he also said something else: that I shouldn't be working for another person, I should be striking out on my own. He would invest, he said, in the next business I started. That business was Bandzie, the predecessor of Fanbytes. True to his word, he made a token investment. But he also did something more important: he introduced me to his own main investor.

The investor in question was a big deal. He's worth hundreds of millions of dollars, he's on a first-name basis with Bill Gates and he was the initial investor in many successful startups. He also became one of our early investors. Meeting him and having his name associated with our company was a massive thing for us. It lent us credibility and unlocked future investment. It was exactly the sort of moment that those entrepreneurs I'd read about would call 'lucky'.

Call it lucky if you like, but that luck was a direct result of me humbly going out into the marketplace several years earlier with the intention to learn about business from those who knew more than I did.

Another important moment was meeting one of our main investors, a guy called Jorg. He was also worth hundreds of millions and was always on hand to bankroll us. Fanbytes simply wouldn't have continued to scale without him. Meeting him might be seen as a stroke of luck. In our second year of business, we did a campaign for a company called TuneMoji, a music messaging app. Through our work with them, they became the number-one trending app in the US. Their CEO was super-hyped and offered to put us in touch with one of their main investors. This was Jorg. He saw the work we'd done with one of his portfolio companies, took an interest in us and ultimately became our biggest investor. From the outside, it must undoubtedly have appeared that luck was on our side.

In reality, Jorg's investment was a by-product of our own hard work.

Even picking Fanbytes as a business included an element of what might externally seem like luck. When we started out as Bandzie, trying to connect bands to their fans through cool experiences, we stumbled upon a YouTuber called Jake West. He was one of the few clients whose audience actually engaged with the concept and bought the merch, and it was only by stumbling upon him that we realized it was the YouTubers who held the influence, as opposed to bands and artists. It felt like a random moment of luck, but of course there was more to it than that. We encountered Jake because we put ourselves out there. It was a function of our previous efforts.

The same could be said more generally for Fanbytes as a concept. From an outside perspective, it seemed serendipitous that we should have a social-media marketing business at the time when social media was booming. In fact, the skills I'd learned when I was much younger – internet marketing and copywriting, public speaking, putting together sales decks – had all compounded, and Fanbytes was the business that best utilized that skill set. Some people might call it luck. Others might join the dots.

Luck is what happens when we focus on the inputs rather than the outputs. We can't always predict precisely what the outputs are going to be, any more than I could have predicted that we'd raise investments from such major players. What we can do is predict that the more we put ourselves out there, the luckier we're likely to be.

Make asymmetric bets

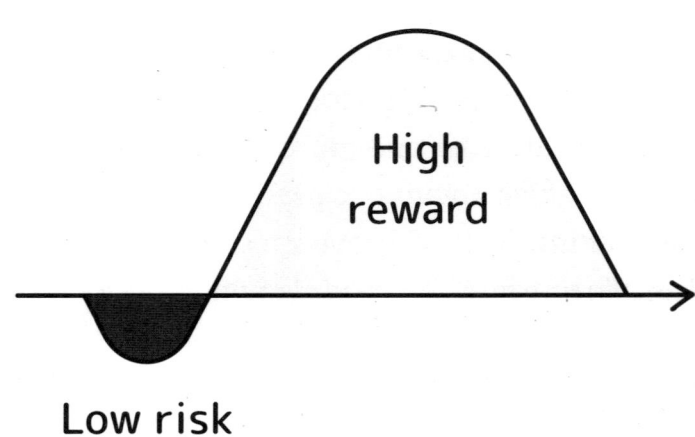

People are obsessed with risk, and particularly of the downside of making risky decisions. 'Leaving my job will be risky, because I may not get another one.' 'Starting this business is risky, because it might fail.' 'Ending this relationship is risky, because I might not find another partner.' And it's true: all these choices come with a hefty dose of risk. We're going to find that our luck is in short supply if we thoughtlessly make risky decisions all the time. Equally, though, we'll never progress if we try to eliminate all element of risk from our lives.

The solution is to place more emphasis on asymmetric bets. An asymmetric bet is a decision where the outcome has very limited – or at least capped – downsides, and almost unlimited upsides. Think of a casino. If you play roulette and believe that, over time, you're going to beat the house, you'll end up poor because that's a wildly asymmetric bet on the part of the casino. They know that, over time, they're going to win. You might not be able to achieve casino levels of certainty in your risk-taking, but you can learn something from this mindset. The notion of the asymmetric bet is common in the world of finance. When an investor makes a small investment in a promising start-up, for example, their losses are limited to the size of that investment, whereas the returns are potentially massive. We can take this idea of asymmetric bets and apply it to our own lives. In fact, much of the advice in this book has this concept at its core.

When we learn a new skill, there is no downside and potentially unlimited upside. Your ability to use that skill productively and improve your own sense of self will always add value to your life. In fact, the obverse is true: by *not* learning new skills, we present ourselves with no upsides and all the potential downsides of failing to open up new perspectives on the world. Learning new skills is an asymmetric bet that will unquestionably increase your chances of a lucky break.

The idea of founding a business with very low start-up costs is another great asymmetric bet. You reap the potential benefit of a successful business – maybe you'll reach financial freedom, you'll certainly learn a bunch of new skills, meet a bunch of new people and have a bunch of new experiences – without the potential drawback of losing funds and time if it doesn't work out.

In chapter four, we talked about building a network. Networking is an obvious asymmetric bet that puts you on the fast track to good fortune. No downside, unlimited upside. The same goes for publishing content online: it's easy to do and costs you nothing, but establishes you as an authoritative voice.

Of course, the value of asymmetric bets is not

limited to the world of business. We can also apply them to our personal lives. The potential downsides of exercise, for example, are almost non-existent. The potential upsides, from the perspective of physical and mental health, confidence and appearance are unlimited. And how many people fail to strike up a conversation with someone they find attractive? This is normally because they fear the fleeting sting of rejection, at the expense of – who knows? – finding a partner for life.

If we make a high volume of asymmetric bets, chances are we'll lose much of the time. But when we win, we win big. To other people, our success will seem like blind luck. But it isn't, because luck, at the micro level, is not about waiting for fate randomly to deal us a decent hand. It's about stacking the deck firmly in our favour.

> 'Every day you get up, you are healthy, and have a packed day ahead – where you can make money, make motion, and build your life [. . .] Be excited. You *get to do this* – You have an opportunity. You are one of the luckiest people on earth.'
> Dr Julie Gurner

Increasing the surface area of luck

You've probably heard it said that luck is where opportunity meets preparation. Imagine two intersecting circles. One of them is your circle of opportunity. The other is your circle of preparation. We can think of luck as being the intersection of these two circles.

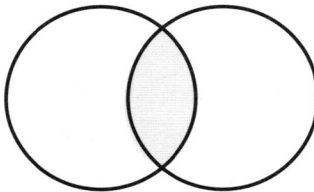

So, how do we increase the surface area of that intersection? It's obvious – we increase the surface area of the two circles.

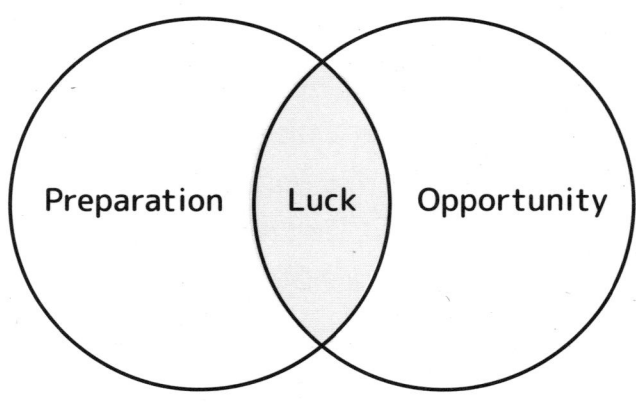

So the question now becomes: how do we increase our circle of preparation and our circle of opportunity? The answer lies in stacking our skills and saying yes until you can say no.

Stack your skills

New skills are easier to learn now than they have ever been. It doesn't matter how old you are, or how experienced. There's always more to learn and we all have access to innumerable resources to help us. We increase our circle of preparation by stacking new skills that have value in the world of work – marketing, perhaps, or negotiation – and then regularly practising them, so when opportunity comes along, we're properly prepared to meet it.

Say yes until you can say no

People often preach the doctrine of focus, especially early on in the game. The more you focus and really drill down into specific actions, the more opportunity will come your way.

I take a different view. I think the doctrine of focus is too narrow. Focus has its place, of course, but it's overrated. Honing in on just one aspect of business or life restricts opportunity. A smarter behaviour is to *keep saying yes until you can say no*. Shots on goal and opportunities for success only happen when you say yes to a lot more things. Meet as many people as possible. Experience as many challenging new scenarios as you can, even if you don't immediately imagine they'll be your cup of tea. Concentrate on breadth rather than depth. Saying yes to everything that comes your way means you meet more people, create more connections and generally increase the circle of opportunity. If you keep saying yes, opportunities *will* come your way. Eventually the moment will arrive when you have so many different, interesting opportunities available to you that you can afford to say no to some of them.

Even now that I'm quote-unquote 'successful', I still make a point of saying yes as much as I can. I never really regret it and I'm often glad I did. I recently bumped into an old friend in a coffee shop. She told me she was about to head off to a hippy-sounding business retreat in Egypt. It sounded like exactly the kind of woo-woo I would normally avoid, but when she invited me, I said yes. And I won't lie: when I first arrived I thought it was pretty lame. During my time there, however, I met two people with whom I created profound connections, one of them personally, the other professionally. The opportunity to meet these people simply wouldn't have come my way if saying 'yes' had not been my default setting.

If we do make saying yes our default setting, it means we can tweak our observation that luck is where opportunity meets preparation. It becomes the case that luck is where preparation meets reality. All we have to do is focus on the things we can control. Eventually the right moment will catch up with us.

> In chapter seven, I told you about how I used to keep an 'I' counter, in order to identify the number of times I used the word 'I' and cut down on it. How about using a yes counter, for the opposite purpose: to positively discriminate in favour of saying yes, and so to increase the number of times you say it. A yes counter helps you concentrate on positivity, on widening your network and your circle of opportunity. When you do this, good things happen.

'Chance favours the prepared mind.'
Louis Pasteur

Be generous

When I was younger, I used to hear people preaching the gospel of generosity: that the more generous you are, the luckier you become. I thought it was one of those pieces of advice that sounded good but was actually a bit meh. It was too wishy-washy and a bit counter-intuitive. I've since learned that it's true: generosity makes good things happen. If you keep giving, it's very hard not to get.

So, what do we mean by generosity? It's not just a question of distributing money, although that can pay dividends. It can be as simple as giving your time or your mental energy to help another person. If you exhibit this behaviour for long enough, you tend to find that you'll win people over and that they'll want to reciprocate. The more you show respect, appreciation and interest towards others, the more they'll do so in return. They'll support your endeavours and cooperate with your wishes. It creates a mutually beneficial cycle of trust.

This is not just wishful thinking. There is a psychological study that measured how well customers tipped their serving staff in a restaurant, according to how many after-dinner sweets the server supplied. The study found a positive correlation between the provision of sweets and the tips. When two sweets were provided, the tips were higher than when only one sweet was provided. But the tips increased dramatically when the server provided one sweet, walked away and then – as if overcome by a moment of generosity – returned to the table and offered another.

This reciprocity principle is sometimes used with a degree of cynicism, of course. The free sample at the supermarket is not offered out of the goodness of the retailer's heart. The Christmas hamper from a client has an obvious ulterior motive. When I say that we should be generous, I'm not suggesting that our attempts at generosity should be quite this sneaky. People aren't stupid and they can distinguish between the genuine and the affected. They know when they're being played. I'm suggesting that adopting a mindset of real generosity can improve the lives of everyone in your circle of influence. Tiny gestures matter. I make a point of recording the birthdays of my friends and acquaintances, and sending them some small, thoughtful token when their birthday comes around. I don't do this because I expect anything in return or because I'm trying to engineer a reciprocal arrangement. I do it because I've learned that the act of generosity not only improves my own wellbeing, it improves the wellbeing of everyone around me. It's not a contrived mindset, but it does open up ways for others to act similarly. When goodwill exists in abundance, great things happen. Reciprocated generosity increases the surface area of luck for everybody involved.

The Cheat Sheet

- Asymmetric bets, with limited downsides and unlimited upsides, stack the deck in our favour.
- Luck is built on a foundation of hard work, self-investment and seeking out opportunities.
- To increase the surface area of luck, we need to increase the surface areas of preparation and opportunity.
- The more generous we are, the luckier we get, because generosity is naturally reciprocated.

Cheatcode 11: Everything Big Starts Small

I have an old diary entry that states my business aim at the time: to build the company to a £1 million annual turnover, then sell it to Snapchat for £4 million. In retrospect, it was a tiny dream. And we started out at a tiny scale. The first campaign we ever sold was to an outdoor activity company. For that campaign we charged £300.

So let's do the maths. At £300 per campaign, we would have needed to sell 3,333 campaigns a year. Sixty-four campaigns a week. Wasn't going to happen.

I never doubted, deep down, that we would get to our seven-figure target. My self-belief was strong. But the size of the job ahead of us was daunting. I couldn't help comparing myself to all the successful business people in my world who seemed to have cracked the code. And I couldn't help but feel slightly overwhelmed by the question of *how* we were going to achieve our goal. We were so small, and our target was so big.

Now, we've spoken earlier in the book about the difficulty of seeing other people apparently so much further ahead than us in business. We've acknowledged that, no matter how strong our self-belief, the sense of not yet being quite there can overwhelm us. We've discussed how we can deploy certain techniques, such as not comparing our internal with other people's external, or focusing on the Gain rather than the Gap, to keep our sense of perspective. Perhaps the most powerful tool we have, however, when we're dealing with the anxiety and frustration of not being where we want to be is to reframe our understanding of what it means to be small. We need to internalize the truth not only that everything big tends to start small, but also that being small offers many advantages that can easily be overlooked, and that incremental progress often trumps giant leaps. In discussing this, I'm going to share some very tactical business strategies that you can easily deploy, whatever stage your business is at.

EVERYTHING BIG STARTS SMALL

Big is not necessarily beautiful

In Cheatcode 5, I talked about the two-step framework. This is the idea that when seeking advice in business, you should target those people who are just a couple of steps ahead of you, rather than those whose businesses are many times bigger than yours. You may recall that I asked advice from a successful entrepreneur and life coach who urged me to think globally. Taking his advice would have been terminal for my business. To have expanded Fanbytes without the proper business infrastructure would simply have been unsustainable. We would have become one more in a long line of businesses who made the critical error of burdening themselves with high costs and operational complexities that they weren't in a position to manage.

It's easy to fall into the trap of wanting to be too big too soon. The path to entrepreneurial success is littered with the corpses of businesses that overreached themselves. Here are some examples of companies for whom this mistake has proved fatal. Let them be a cautionary tale.

Crumbs Bake Shop

Back in the early 2000s, when cupcakes were having a bit of a moment, Crumbs was the largest cupcake vendor in the United States. It was founded in 2003 in Manhattan by a husband-and-wife team, and it was a huge hit. It then quickly expanded multiple product lines into multiple cities, but the expansion was unsustainable, not only because of the high cost of maintaining dozens of retail outlets but also because – after a cupcake bubble – the craze for cupcakes started to decline. The momentum was impossible to sustain and the company encountered real difficulties. Happily, in recent years, they've managed to relaunch themselves, but theirs is a cautionary tale: when you expand too quickly based on over-optimistic assumptions about a product's future viability in the marketplace (cupcakes are nice to have but don't solve a particular market need), you make problems for yourself.

Zynga

Zynga offered free video games at a time when the market was full of low-quality examples of the genre. It started off well and, with cash in the bank, spent $100 million on its own data centres and $228 million on a headquarters in San Francisco. But the company couldn't innovate as quickly as it expanded, and it soon had to lay off staff and close down those data centres. It still exists as a company, but at a much smaller scale, having spent eye-watering sums on premature growth.

pets.com

Founded in 1998, pets.com aimed to harness the burgeoning e-commerce market in the valuable niche of pet supplies. A good idea. It attracted substantial investment and almost instant popularity. It expanded fast but encountered high operating costs and marketing expenses, while competitors ate into its market share. The company's expansion took place at the expense of proper strategic planning and an awareness of the need to find a balance between growth and stability.

The list of companies that failed because they tried to run before they could walk is long. It's understandable that founders should wish rapid growth for their businesses, because successful growth is the path to wealth. Big can be beautiful, and scaleable businesses are the holy grail if you want a high-value exit, but sometimes we need to temper our desire to expand too quickly by considering the advantages of being small. This means being open to a change of mindset.

Reframing small

I'm not here to tell you that you shouldn't strive to expand. This cheatcode is Everything Big Starts Small, not Everything Small Has To Stay Small. The point is to avoid looking with disdain at where we are, to embrace those times in business when we're small and to focus on the benefits of smallness rather than constantly obsessing about the need to be bigger. Being big comes with its own set of problems, and you're far better placed to deal with those problems when you've encountered them at a smaller scale.

The fetishization of the large is a very human trait. We all want bigger houses, bigger cars, bigger bank balances. For entrepreneurs, the ultimate aim is to be a big company. We see big as 'good' and small as 'bad'. I've learned that this is a flawed way of thinking, especially in business. I like to use the analogy of a speedboat and a yacht. A yacht is certainly the most impressive. It's grand and comfortable, an ostentatious display of wealth for those who yearn for recognition. None of that can really be said for a speedboat. But what happens when our vessels suddenly and urgently need to change course? The yacht changes course slowly and gently – some might even say clumsily. The speedboat? The change of course is done in a matter of seconds. It has a level of speed and agility that the yacht simply can't achieve on account of its size. What's true for seafaring vessels is true for businesses. When you're small, you have the ability to move fast. You're not weighed down by the complexities of your systems. You can pivot and change trajectory with ease. And owning a speedboat is fun! (There's a reason people return to startups after a successful exit.)

Document your small wins

I wish that when Fanbytes was in its infancy, I'd taken the opportunity to document our small wins. The earliest picture I have of the Fanbytes team was taken after we'd expanded to 40 people. I regret not having anything earlier than that. Building a business is as much about the journey as the destination – again, that's why entrepreneurs often repeatedly start new ventures even when they don't need the money. By making a conscious effort to document the small wins, we force ourselves to focus on the journey by creating memories, and so we enjoy the process more. It also helps us to appreciate the progress we're making, rather than constantly thinking with anxiety about the endgame. It puts the emphasis firmly on the Gain rather than the Gap.

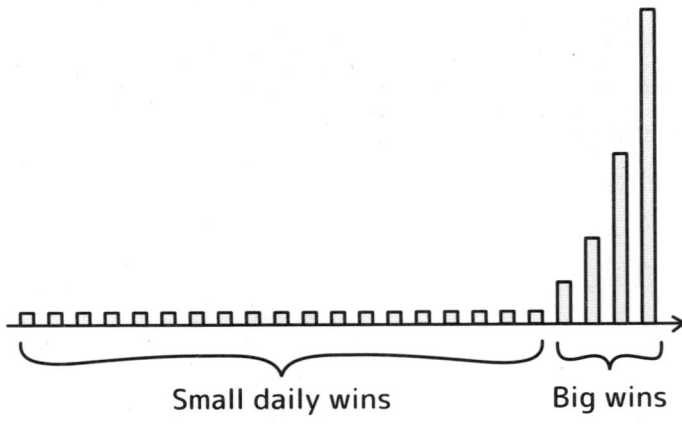

Small daily wins   Big wins

And if that sounds a bit fluffy for you, there is a more concrete psychological advantage to this approach. When you document the early incremental stages of growth, it helps you keep a sense of perspective when those increases start to feel bigger and scarier. You're going to deal much better with that moment when your business increases to a turnover of £100,000, if you're able to look back with clarity to when it was turning over

£10,000, which probably felt scary in itself. You're able to say to yourself: this is just like that other time, but with an extra zero!

> If you're serious about your goal, make sure every day gets you slightly closer. You think you were relaxing for a few days. Then it becomes a few months. Then a few years. A bad workout is better than no workout. A cold email out is better than no email out. A page a day is better than no pages a day. Momentum is a hell of a drug. When you've got it, don't let it slip.

How do we get a quick win?

Everything big starts small, but momentum matters. Rather than resigning yourself to the necessity of grinding away for a week, a month or even longer before chalking up a positive result, you'll get a much better sense of momentum if you're on the hunt for a quick win. It may be that your win aligns with a traditional marker of success – a new customer, perhaps, or a repeat sale. We can hack our sense of momentum, though, by changing our markers of success. A marker of success might be speaking to ten potential clients about your lunchtime sandwich business in a two-day period. Quick win, even if you don't close a deal with any of them. A marker of success might be writing the first five slides of your sales deck. Quick win, even if you haven't yet made a presentation. The point is to give yourself a framework that encourages constant forward motion. If we continue making incremental improvements, success becomes simply a function of time. But time can drag, and concentrating on small, quick wins keeps us motivated while we're waiting for the big, slow wins to come along.

The three Cs of compounding

There is an old mathematical parable about the power of exponential growth. In this parable, a man invents the game of chess and presents it to a powerful king. Delighted with the game, the king wants to reward him. The man chooses an apparently humble reward: one grain of rice for the first square on the chess board, two for the second, four for the third and so on, the amount of rice doubling with each square. The king grants his request, unaware that the power of exponential growth means that the man will receive more than 9 million million million grains on the 64th square.

That's the power of compounding. It's an important concept in finance, where small, regular yields, properly reinvested, appreciate over time and provide large returns. It's an important concept in business strategy, too. I knew that Fanbytes would not grow to the size I hoped if all we did was attempt to replicate the £300 campaign for the outdoor activity company. We would have to harness the power of compounding. This was not simply a question of gradually increasing our fees, although that was part of it. We had to consider what I call the three Cs of compounding: cost, confidence and clients.

Cost

We'd never have made it if we only ever charged £300. The mathematics didn't work. It was very obvious that to scale up the business, we needed to scale up our fees. As the fees increased, the number of contracts we needed to reach a certain level reduced. If we'd asked for £100,000 for our first contract, however, we'd soon have got into trouble. We had no concept of the value of our product, what our customers wanted to pay or what they would expect for their money. The secret lay in regular incremental increases as we understood our own service better, and as we increased in the second C, confidence.

Confidence

Asking for money can be hard and it can be scary. We had to be confident in our ability to ask for, and fulfil, a £300 contract before we could hope to have the confidence to ask for a £700 contract. We had to be confident in our ability to ask for and fulfil a £700 contract before we had the confidence to ask for £1,000. The compounding of confidence is crucial in business and one of the principal reasons why big enterprises should start small. As confidence compounds, momentum builds. Everything big starts small, but it's also true that what once seemed big will soon seem small.

Clients

A single client is a good start but a bad finish. They have limited money to spend and can easily take their business away (or go out of business themselves). You've no real hope of scaling your business if you don't focus on gradually compounding your client base. Again, incremental increases are key: too many clients too soon will likely lead you to overcommit and underdeliver – a brilliant way to become one of the failed businesses at the start of this chapter. Starting from a small base gives you the ability to widen your reach at a sustainable rate.

Give yourself room to grow

We were grateful for our first contract with the outdoor activity company, but in retrospect they were a terrible first client to choose. Everything big starts small, but if you want to compound your client base, you need to ensure that there are other clients within the same sector to whom you can expand your services. In our case, there were no other similar companies for whom we could use our work as a case study. It was an early lesson in the importance, when you're small, of carefully choosing specific customer segments when considering your plans to grow.

In our case, things really started to move when we switched our focus to record labels. We did a Snapchat campaign with a major record label for a song by a well known artist. We charged £1,000 for the campaign, and it drummed up an impressive amount of engagement, views and streams. On the back of that success, we were able to approach a rival label, and they engaged us to do a similar campaign for another famous pop star. We had the confidence to ask for £3,000 for that campaign, and having started with one small client in a big pond, we were then in a position to present our services to other record labels and offer them meaningful data to support our claims for the service.

Everything big starts small, but it's important that in your early endeavours you're thinking strategically about how to scale up to the next level. You need room to grow.

The client ascension strategy

At the beginning of Fanbytes, we would go directly to customers and ask them if they wanted to buy an influencer campaign. Simple as that. This was not an effective technique. It barely ever worked and our close rate was minimal.

So we changed our approach, as we were able to do quickly because we were small. We pivoted to what I call the client ascension strategy. The idea behind this strategy is to get your client to commit to something small, then gradually to increase the scale of their commitment, to the point where you've established your authority and the potential value of your service to them. The relationship starts small, and grows.

In the case of Fanbytes, we would encourage a potential client to engage with us by giving them a free ebook about the influencer landscape. It required little of them, least of all money, but provided something of interest and put us on their radar. Next, we'd invite them to a webinar where they could come online for 15 or 20 minutes and learn about how their competitors were making use of the influencer space. Again, it required little in the way of commitment, but consolidated us as a trusted authority. Then we'd invite them to a free event, where they'd have the opportunity to spend an hour or so with us and really strengthen the relationship. When we pitched customers cold, it was hardly surprising that so few of them were interested. They'd have to take a vast leap of faith. But when somebody goes from giving you five minutes of their time, to 15 minutes, to an hour, they take a far smaller leap in deciding they want to work with you when you ask them.

The client ascension strategy – which can be adapted to almost any business – took us from a 10 per cent close rate to a 75 per cent close rate. It was simply a question of scaling our potential clients' confidence in us incrementally. That confidence started small but ended big.

Focus on marginal gains

The theory of marginal gains was popularized in sport by the cycling coach Dave Brailsford. The concept focuses on small but consistent improvements across various aspects of performance, which cumulatively lead to significant progress. For example, if a sportsperson makes an improvement of a percentage point in their training, sleep and nutrition respectively, the cumulative effect can be substantial. The whole becomes more than the sum of its parts.

Allow me to put my Tim's Tutors hat on, because there's some maths at work here. I'm going to introduce you to what I call the rule of 10 per cent. Let's imagine we have a business or service with 1,000 clients, whose average order value is £100 and who buy twice per year. Our annual revenue will be:

1,000 x £100 x 2 = £200,000

Now, let's say that we try to increase each of these components by a small, manageable amount, say 10 per cent. That's not too big an ask. It will give us 1,100 clients, paying an average of £110, buying an average of 2.2 times per year. Under this scenario, our annual revenue will be:

1,100 x £110 x 2.2 = £266,200

Those small, marginal gains of 10 per cent in the individual components of the business lead to an overall gain of 33 per cent in total revenue. For the maths geeks out there, this is just a practical application of the fact that 1.1 x 1.1 x 1.1 = 1.331. For everybody else, it's an illustration that instead of focusing on optimizing a big number by a large amount, we should focus on optimizing small components by achievable multiples. This is a much easier, much more effective strategy. Like the cyclists who focus on marginal gains in fitness, nutrition and equipment to achieve a substantial overall improvement in performance, so the business owner who focuses on marginal gains across the business will benefit from a compounding effect.

Control the controllables

In my early days with the business, I found myself confused. I couldn't confidently say what I thought the business would do in the next month or two. I sure as hell couldn't tell you what we were going to do in the next quarter. We were hitting targets, but I wasn't quite certain how. I knew things might work out, but they very well might not. I understood the power of compounding, but I wasn't totally sure which variables were having an active effect on our growth, and which weren't.

I looked back on our most successful months and saw a correlation between the small actions we could control and the wider success. I looked at how many emails we sent, I looked at how many leads we followed, I looked at our sales conversion numbers. When these numbers were high, we saw a corresponding uptick in our fortunes. I decided, from that point on, that I would only worry about the inputs that were in our power to influence, rather than the outputs that weren't. I would, in short, control the controllable.

We've learned the importance of focusing on the inputs rather than the outputs. Too often we over-focus on the big picture instead of the details that comprise it. The big picture, though, is out of our control, or rather it is a function of the smaller inputs that we provide. I decided that instead of thinking: How are we going to do a hundred grand this month? We should be thinking: How many calls are we going to make this month? Or how many conferences are we going to attend? Everything big starts small when we make a conscious effort to control the controllables because by definition, the controllables are the small things. They are the ten-second reach-outs to somebody on social media; the five-minute phone call to a new prospect; the hour you spend creating a presentation for a client. They are the tiny actions that we can actively take to make incremental progress, and so benefit from a compounding effect.

You will never be ready

A few years ago, I was being interviewed by a BBC reporter who asked me if I had any closing thoughts about how to make it in business. The closing thought that popped straight into my head was this: you will never be ready. The time will probably never arrive when the stars are completely aligned. The cards will never all be stacked in your favour. There was never a moment when I was suddenly 'ready' to start public speaking or 'ready' to ask for large sums of money.

The secret lies in taking the smallest possible action to put you closer to your goal. We've talked about taking the path of least resistance, and that mindset applies here. When we're overwhelmed by the vastness of our ambition and the realization that we'll never be fully ready, the smallest actions take on much greater importance. Those small actions quickly accumulate and compound. They mitigate your lack of preparedness and stop you from becoming paralysed into inactivity by the fact that you do not feel ready to take larger strides.

Minimum viable product vs minimum viable step

In business, people talk about having the minimum viable product, or MVP. An MVP is the simplest version of a product, with sufficient features to test an idea in the marketplace but not so much complexity that it should require unrealistic levels of expense or resources before its wider viability has been confirmed. The MVP strategy is an effective way to avoid the bloat and jeopardy of starting too big too soon. As well as allowing you to test the product before overcommitting to it, it gives you the opportunity to learn from early-stage feedback and to make iterative improvements.

Here are some examples of big businesses that started small using the concept of an MVP.

Dropbox

This popular file synchronization platform initially launched as a simple video demo, which showcased its technology. This allowed the founders to judge demand before building out the platform on a vast scale.

Groupon

This started out as a blog advertising deals. When the founders received enough interest for a deal, they'd send out coupons. This MVP validated the theory that a demand existed for group-buying deals without the need to roll out a full platform.

Deliveroo

Deliveroo started out by delivering only to a small area of London, establishing the market need and the logistical feasibility of the concept before expanding it across the country.

When I started Tim's Tutors back in school, I was my own MVP. Having established that there was a market need for tutoring services among my peers, I was then able to expand my core service accordingly. If you're starting a new business, there's no doubt that the minimum viable product concept could be a useful strategy. Let's imagine you want to start a pet-grooming service where you'll collect and deliver the pets (which is a good idea for a business, by the way). You could rent premises, take out a lease on a van, buy all the grooming equipment, design fancy logos and signage, create a fully functioning website, and hire a couple of members of staff. Or you could create a simple landing page with a form where customers can book a grooming session and a pick-up, and advertise your services on local Facebook groups. One strategy will cost you a fortune up front with absolutely no guarantee of a penny in revenue. The other strategy will get your business up and running quickly, and without much jeopardy. Most importantly, it will test the market need. It may be that people are crying out for this service in your area. It might be a dud. You won't know until you've dipped your toe in the water.

So, the minimum viable product is a successful and well-established strategy. Hopefully its value is clear when we consider the concept that everything big starts small. But I also want to encourage you to tweak it so that it's even simpler, and to consider a strategy that I call the minimum viable action. The MVA is the smallest step you can take to get an idea out of your head and into the world. In the case of the pet-grooming service, the minimum viable action might be to fire up Google and see how many pet-grooming services there are in your immediate neighbourhood. It might be a conversation with another dog-walker in the park, assessing their enthusiasm for the idea. It might be sitting down of an evening to make a list of prices. These are tiny steps that could only take two or three minutes. They involve no interaction with a customer. They don't even involve the creation of a core product. They are foundation stones, almost imperceptible movements towards a far-off goal, but deliberate ones. A journey of a thousand miles begins with a single step. The minimum viable action is that step. Too many business ideas stay in the brains of those who think them up. The MVA gets them out of your brain and into the world.

Time is the ultimate decider

We can see that small things become big when we consider the compounding effect of incremental improvements; when we maintain steady forward momentum; when we document the small wins and hustle for quick ones. It becomes very difficult not to win when you consistently keep improving like this. This is as true for chefs or musicians or football players as it is for entrepreneurs, and it allows us to reframe our thinking whenever we become overwhelmed by the question of how we're going to reach our end target. It means, so long as we have the right systems in place, that the arbiter of success is simply time. The question becomes not *will* I be successful, but *when* will I be successful. If you've chosen the right skill and you've chosen the right market and you're constantly improving, then, barring some disastrous turn of unforeseen events, you will eventually win.

The Cheat Sheet

- Big is not necessarily beautiful. Small can be. This mindset helps us avoid the tendency to resent where we currently are, and not to overreach ourselves too soon.
- When we document our small wins, we assign value to the journey and help ourselves keep perspective when the milestones become bigger.
- It's OK to be small, but you need room to grow.

- Harness the power of compounding through incremental improvements and marginal gains. When you make small optimizations in many areas of your business, the total optimization is large.
- By definition, you can't control the uncontrollable. So when you make a choice to control the controllables, you force yourself to activate the compounding effect of marginal gains.
- Take the minimum viable step to get a business idea out of your head and into the world.
- When the correct systems are in place at a micro level, and barring unforeseen disasters, bigger success simply becomes a function of time.

Afterword

We are the stories we tell ourselves. As a young boy, I used to climb the concrete stairwell of our council block on the Old Kent Road, repeating a mantra in my head: I don't belong here. I'm meant for more. I wanted to be the one in my family who broke the generational chain of poverty, but although I had a very clear idea of the destination, I didn't know how I was going to make the journey. The path was hidden. I had to work out the best way of finding it.

And I did. On 3 May 2022, a sum of money landed in my bank account that would redefine my future. That money comprised the proceeds that came from a successful business exit. And that successful business exit happened because, over time, I came to understand the principles that I've explained in these cheatcodes. They quite literally changed my life.

I wanted to share the cheatcodes far and wide, but I never had any real intention to write a book. Why would

AFTERWORD

I, when I knew that I could make online content that would be seen by millions of people within a week? In time, though, I came to realize that if I could give my 21-year-old self a gift, this would be it: a book that dug a little deeper and detailed all the hard-won truths I'd learned in my time building a successful business. I hope that this gift to my former self has also been of value to you, whether you're a young entrepreneur, whether you're further along in your journey, or even if you want to achieve an outcome that is not directly related to entrepreneurship but which might benefit from the strategies and mindsets that I've found so helpful in my own life. The cheatcodes are flexible and have applications far beyond the world of business.

I also hope that in reading this book, you will have come to the realization – just as I have – that the people who have achieved the goals to which you aspire are not really any different to the rest of us. They don't have two heads. They just have a way of looking at the world which has helped them. If you can look at the world similarly, and compare your inputs with their inputs, it can help you, too. The cheatcodes are a way of re-framing how we approach both business and life. So if you're a person who knows they're meant for more – just as I did all those years ago as I climbed that concrete

AFTERWORD

stairwell – I hope that they will set you on the path to where you want to be and make the journey easier, faster and ultimately more fulfilling.

So go out there and rewrite your story. You have the tools to do it. Now all you have to do is put them into action.

Acknowledgements

To Ambrose, Mitchell and Lucy, for putting up with my B.S.

To Adam Parfitt, for the constant WhatsApp voice notes and for making this a fun process.

To Corinna Bolino, Katya Browne, Olimpia Southgate-Smith, Ellie Crisp, Shunayna Vaghela, Serena Nazareth and all at Michael Joseph.

To Kate Evans and all at PFD.

Thanks for helping me make this book a reality.

List of Sources

p. 76, James Clear, *Atomic Habits: An Easy & Proven Way to Build Good Habits & Break Bad Ones* (Random House Business, 2018)

p. 85, Bruce Lee © Bruce Lee Enterprises, LLC. All rights reserved

p. 106, Seneca, *Epistles, Volume I: Epistles 1–65*, trs Richard M. Gummere, Loeb Classical Library 75 (Harvard University Press, 1917)

p. 109, Kerry McCarthy, 'Usain Bolt: The Fastest Man on Earth', *Runner's World* (5 July 2011)

p. 125, Albert Bigelow Paine, *Mark Twain: A Biography: The Personal and Literary Life of Samuel Langhorne Clemens*, vol. 3 (Harper & Bros, 1912)

p. 131, *This Is Working with Daniel Roth*, 'Former President Barack Obama on working' (June 2023)

p. 154, Bianna Golodryga, *Good Morning America* interview with Warren Buffett, ABC (10 July 2009)

LIST OF SOURCES

pp. 165–6, Chet Holmes, *The Ultimate Sales Machine: Turbocharge Your Business with Relentless Focus on 12 Key Strategies* (Penguin, 2007)

pp. 182–3, James Kerr, *Legacy: What the All Blacks Can Teach Us About the Business of Life* (Constable, 2013)

p. 187, Richard P. Feynman, 'Cargo Cult Science', commencement address, Caltech, Pasadena, USA (4 June 1974)

p. 207, Roger Federer, commencement address, Dartmouth College, Hanover, USA (9 June 2024)

p. 213, Alice Schroeder, *The Snowball: Warren Buffett and the Business of Life* (Bloomsbury, 2008)

p. 247, Dr Julie Gurner, post on X (6 September 2024)

p. 251, Louis Pasteur, inaugural lecture, University of Lille, France (7 December 1854)